WANSEA BOY

To Dorothy
with love
Alun
Sept 2014

A SWANSEA BOY

Alun John Richards

ISBN: 978–1-84524-201-5

Cover design: Lynwen Jones

Gwasg Carreg Gwalch, Llanrwst
☏: 01758 750432 ℻: 01758 750438
✉: books@carreg-gwalch.com
Website: www.carreg-gwalch.com

Introduction

I was born in Swansea in 1924, sharing a birthday with such diverse notables as W. G. Grace, Nelson Mandela, Vidkun Quisling and George (Machine Gun) Kelly.

I have tried to maintain a child's perspective where everything was fresh, new and it never rained and adults existed in a parallel universe.

My father's forebears were Carmarthenshire Blacksmiths and Ministers, it being said that those lacking the wit to be one became the other, although which way round, I do not know.

My mother's folk were Norfolk shoemakers until they said 'Cobblers to that' and took up farming. Claiming descent from Oliver Cromwell's cousin, her politics were mildly radical. It is probably a common adherence to the Liberal Party that brought them together.

They made an odd couple, he was reassuringly portly, be-monocled and watch-chained with the gravitias of a bon vivant, while she was small and slight like an underfed ferret. He was as placid as she was fiery, so as when two rip tides merge, the waters were often choppy.

They attempted to inculcate in me senses of thrift, honesty and prudence, fortunately without total success since such traits are a serious handicap in the modern world.

Acknowledgements

In this quest of the past, I have been aided by dear and doughty folk such as Anita Baker, Denise Billington, Ashley Bowen, Bliss Brimley, Billie Carnes, Caroline Clarke, Pamela Dorey, Jeanette Drew, David Evans, David & Edward Hitchings, Elizabeth Jones, Gareth Wyn-Jones, Maureen Griffith Jones, John & David Kett, Maureen Ledbury, John & Richard Lowrie, Frances & Isobel Oliver, Roberta Thomas, Rose Tinsley and Siân Williams who share my gene pool. Plus others such as David Morris, Pam Pearce, Reece Webb, the staffs of Swansea and Carmarthen Archives and the members of West Dereham Heritage Group, who kindly helped. In mentioning family and friends, I have in general made my 'cut off point' my own generation, partly because they had no influence on my early life and partly because they can in due course make their own record. If I have unfairly traduced anyone I am sorry, but have tried to honour historical accuracy and personal perception.

Alun John Richards,
Swansea 2013

Books by Alun John Richards:

Gazeteer of the Welsh Slate Industry,
ISBN 0-86381-196-5, Gwasg Carreg Gwalch
Slate Quarrying at Corris, ISBN 0-86381-279-1,
Gwasg Carreg Gwalch
Slate Quarrying in Wales, ISBN 0-86381-319-4,
Gwasg Carreg Gwalch
The Slate Quarries of Pembrokeshire, ISBN 0-86381-484-0,
Gwasg Carreg Gwalch
The Slate Regions of North and Mid Wales,
ISBN 0-86381-552-9, Gwasg Carreg Gwalch
Fragments of Mine & Mill, ISBN 0-86381-812-9,
Gwag Carreg Gwalch
The Slate Railways of Wales, ISBN 0-86381-689-4,
Gwasg Carreg Gwalch
Welsh Slate Craft, ISBN 0-84527-029-0, Gwasg Carreg Gwalch
Crefft Llechi, ISBN0-84527-034-7, Gwasg Carreg Gwalch
Slate Quarrying in Corris, ISBN 1-84524-068-5, Llygad Gwalch
Slate Quarrying in Wales (Rev), ISBN 0-84527-026-6,
Gwasg Carreg Gwalch
The Slate Quarries of Pembrokeshire,
ISBN 978-1-84524-189-6, Llygad Gwalch
Tinplate in Wales, ISBN 978-1-84524-125-4, Llygad Gwalch
The Rails & Sails of Welsh Slate, ISBN-9781-84524-174-2,
Llygad Gwlach

With Gwynfor Pierce Jones:
Cwm Gwyrfai, ISBN 0-86381-897-8, Gwasg Carreg Gwalch

With Jean Napier:
A Tale of Two Rivers, ISBN 0-86381-989-3,
Gwasg Carreg Gwalch
Two Snowdonia Rivers, ISBN 978-1-84527-206-7,
Gwasg Carreg Gwalch
The River Conwy, Source to Sea, ISBN 978-1-84527-288-3,
Gwasg Carreg Gwalch

Contents

1

In the Beginning

It would be curmudgeonly to comment on how persons and property were safe on the streets and how shops were pleased to see you and anxious to sell you something you wanted rather than haughtily condescending to interrupt their personal discussions to allow you to buy what they want to get rid of. Nor times when shops were long established specialists staffed by knowledgeable assistants and not by insolent 'Sales Advisors'. Nor the times when banks were honest with managers whom one could trust and confide in, nor Building Societies who recorded transactions in a ledger which was never 'Down', nor grocers that provided you with a chair not a trolley.

Nor am I going to go on about how a clean, unvandalised telephone box on almost every street corner made mobile phones unnecessary, or that cars could be parked anywhere (Unlocked) confident that it would be still there, undamaged when one returned. In fact until 1930 it was illegal to lock a car and thus prevent it being moved should it prove to be causing someone inconvenience. Enough has been said and written about those things.

Churches and chapels that survived both the Blitz and the bulldozers have collapsed under a weight of indifference or have been found uses by other faiths or for secular purposes. Of the latter, conversion to apartments seems the least undesirable although some occupants must find that the ambience inhibits at least the more imaginative marital activities, particularly if the bedroom encompasses say the erstwhile site of the *sêt fawr*. (The raised bench reserved for the Deacons or Elders).

Happily gone is much of the revulsion at the use of Welsh or fear of being recognised as Welsh. It has not all gone – I recall at a dinner in the Home Counties, finding myself sitting next to a Whitehall mandariness whose authoritative Oxford vowels failed to entirely conceal a familiar lilt, creating what might be called a Cwmisis accent. I asked her what part of south Wales she came from. Had I suggested crawling under the table for some seriously indecent purpose, she could not have been more offended. Eventually in a claret-induced recklessness, she grudgingly admitted a slight acquaintance with the Vale of Glamorgan. In the end, after several glasses the posh 'varls' became valley 'vow-wells' and the syntax unmistakably 'Wenglish' and she confessed to being a Morriston girl.

Morriston has lost its importance as the 'Capital of Swansea', but not completely so. Only a few years ago in a train in Italy, I fell into conversation with a Frenchman. He was dressed in what had clearly been a 3-piece suit that was now technically a 2-piece since he had no trousers. As I had noticed him producing a diplomatic passport and his boxer shorts appeared to be expensive I assumed him to be a person of some consequence who had suffered some embarrassing mishap, so I refrained from commenting on his garb. He asked me where I came from, he shrugged with incomprehension when I said Pays de Gales, but after some verbal fencing I admitted to Angleterre.

He said 'London?'

I said 'Swansea.'

He shrugged and after much pondering tried 'Birm-ing-ham?'

In response to my headshake he said 'Glasgow?'

Knowing that even the stupidest foreigner can be made to understand if one shouts loudly enough, I countered with 'CARDDEEFF!!!'

He remained expressionless. So I tried a more subtle approach. Finger-sketching an imaginary map I carefully enunciated

'Trois – cent – et – vingt – kilomètres – précisément – au – Ouest – de - Londres,' emphasising the point with three fingers, omitting to follow with two fingers and a forefinger-thumb circle. Realising that such gestures might be misunderstood I gestured towards the then setting sun.

At last a great grin of comprehension slowly spread across his face 'Ah Morereeston!' adding in a mutter that I took to be the French equivalent of 'Why couldn't you have said so in the first place'.

One's early impressions, opinions and experiences are received second-hand from our parents, as are our views and prejudices. Just as a TV producer directs his shots and plans the programme content to suit his perception of what he thinks you should know, so our input is controlled and conditioned with inevitable partiality. Moreover they select one's name, which to some extent moulds one's whole life. (Could Dr. King the great American civil rights leader have achieved such eminence had he been baptised say George?). My first name defines my nationality – how with my mother's galloping Gallophobia, the Old Man ever got away with that I shall never know – all she could do was to pronounce it as if it were Alan. John was my grandfather's name but my third given name Yorke is a mystery. Apart from being aware that three given names are excessive by anyone's standards, I became so fed up with saying 'There's an ee on Yorke' that I ceased using it.

Therefore any account of oneself must begin with one's parents.

Had I been aware of the word, I would have called my father enigmatic, but then I never really knew him, few did. Some claimed to do so but they generally exposed their falsity by referring to him as 'Tom'. To all, other than his most immediate relatives, he was 'Teedoubleyou' or when deference demanded it, 'Mister Teedoubleyou'. Such widespread adoption of this Welsh custom of creating a forename out of initials when the use of a Christian name seemed presumptuous perhaps emphasises his air of inapproachability.

Being 47 when I was born there was not a generation gap so much as a generation chasm. Our relationship might have been the friendly intimacy of grandfather-grandson, but he was always as uneasy in my company as I was in his. I realise in retrospect the divide was not of generations but of centuries. He was of an era when to have gas lighting was the height of sophistication, he would have been an adult when he saw his first motorcar. He must have been in his twenties before he lived in a house with electric light and pushing forty before he heard a gramophone or saw an aeroplane – he was very much a child of the 19th century – a true Victorian.

He mistrusted most inventions, predicting (usually incorrectly) that they would never catch on and foretelling (usually correctly) that no good would come of them. The telephone was grudgingly tolerated but oddly, the wireless was embraced. Not in the crystal set era – the fine adjustment of the 'Cat's Whisker' would have been beyond him – but when the two-valve set in its oak case arrived; it was draped with a lace doily and treated with the deference due to a household shrine. Every word that croakily emanated from it was treated as Delphically oracular, particularly the weather forecast. If it rained when the wireless had forecast sunshine, he would regard this as a shortcoming of the Almighty rather than of the BBC.

It was of course a battery set, a man called on a Thursday to take away the depleted accumulator and replace it with a recharged one, since this occurred when father was 'at business', precise instructions were always left regarding this vital exchange. This observance ceased when this apparatus was replaced by a 'Radio-gramophone'. Not an HMV nor a Phillips and certainly not an American 'Mid West' favoured by our wealthiest acquaintances, but a locally made lash up, presumably foisted on him by one of his Rotary club friends.

It must have cost at least £20, which even as an employer of almost 30 people and the holder of a modest clutch of investments, would have been as much as he made in a month, but although it was an 'All Mains' contrivance, it was guaranteed that there would be no risk of electrocution. One could 'Tune In' to exotic places such as Luxemburg or Normandy and listen to the jolly children who drank Ovaltine and the happy souls that thrived on Horlicks. Since the BBC's ban on advertising was draconian, there was a frisson of forbidden fruit about such broadcasts.

Unfortunately this particular set brought me no kudos amongst my friends whose fathers had 'Short Wave' that could, crackling and distortedly pick up America. In fact this was the age of the great distance boast, and jokes of the – 'We get Chile with the window open,' variety.

My father unworried by these limitations concentrated on the record-playing potential. Costing up to 6/- (30p – a day's pay for many men), the number of these shining black discs which he alone was allowed to handle, was limited, but his tastes were disparate – John McCormack's Mother Macree, the Londonderry Air, Walford Davies' Solemn Melody, the Laughing Policeman, the Sailor's Hornpipe.

Listening to records, indeed doing anything, work or play, winter or summer, my father's dress was always the same Sidney Heath tailor-made suit with waistcoat. (Not the 8-guinea (£8.40) variety worn by those in the higher echelons of the professions or the 4-guinea worn by clerks, but the sound middle-of-the-road 6-guinea article). It was invariably worn with a blue shirt with stiff white collars. These collars were fresh on every day since a weekly van took away seven soiled collars and delivered seven gleaming newly starched replacements. His boots were big and black and his hat a stiff and uncompromising grey Homburg. Even indoors, even in retirement, sitting glued to the TV staring fixedly at the test card, waiting for the programmes to begin; his garb (including trilby hat) remained unchanged.

Actually The Hat served a vital purpose – as a 'Safety Helmet' when he was indulging in his favourite pastime – chopping firewood. Despite many years experience and some ability at splitting along the grain with the hatchet, the art of shortening the resultant sticks was never mastered. His method was to apply maximum force to the stick with the hatchet. The result usually being that one or more halves would fly high into the air. Thus his cross-chopping was a matter of strike and cower – hence The Hat. The 'Mad Axe man' would have been an appropriate sobriquet. Wooden boxes and packing cases would be included with the 'Goods' delivered from 'The Warehouse' on a Friday afternoon. Thus the weekend could be spent reducing these to manageable sticks for lighting the several fires. Apart from 'The Range', that black leaded behemoth of the kitchen, there was, except perhaps in the warmest weather a fire in 'The Library' as the main living room was somewhat extravagantly called. A fire was lit in the parents' bedroom on cold evenings and on the rare occasions when Company was expected, in 'The Dining

Room' as well. Despite the name and its fine extending table, nothing more than the obligatory 'A cup of tea in the hand' was normally consumed there. The three-piece suite was so signally uncomfortable that guests rarely accepted a second cup and never outstayed their welcome.

My father was of course 'in business' which was apparently the only respectable occupation for a gentleman. Solicitors and accountants and the like had their place but then so had dustmen and other persons who 'went out to work'. He was in fact a wholesale grocer and owned lorries, two great big lumbering Leylands, an Albion, chain driven like some monster motorcycle and the grandpa of them all a Milnes-Daimler. Such vehicles, tall as a house, with vast solid-tyred wheels and two-man starting handles proclaimed that a wholesale grocer was not just a cut but a whole bacon slicerful above an ordinary grocer whose transport was limited to a boy on a bicycle. Just to prove that the firm was no slave to modernity there was also a two-wheeled covered cart drawn by a high stepping roan, which was a sure-fire winner at the annual Swansea Show.

To a child, of course it was sometimes difficult to mentally disassociate 'doing business' and 'doing one's business'; occasionally giving me bizarre images of what went on between 9 and 5.

In his commendable endeavour to interest me in activities that he considered edifying, my father took me to rugby at St Helens, where, he being a Committee member we sat in a reserved section in the middle of the stand. My chief memory is of coruscating cold, and watching persons who, since they wore short trousers I took to be little boys, running about at random and for some reason frequently fell down. This instilled a life-long aversion to football of every kind. In summer at the cricket pavilion things were warmer but just as mysterious and even more boring. There were men in white (grown ups in long trousers) most of whom stood about seemingly not doing anything. A ball would be thrown and hit and someone would run after it and just occasionally the spectators would clap. On one occasion some excitement was promised because the West Indians were playing. I expected a crowd of jolly fellows hitting seven bells out of dustbins, but it proved to be the same boring old cricket.

Of more interest were the visits he took me accompanied by my 'Little chums' to such places as the newspaper offices, the flour mill, the electricity works and suchlike, but these were confined to birthdays which were not occasions of unalloyed happiness since such anniversaries were accompanied by parties. Not that I was averse to jelly and blancmange but I was forced to put up with the son of one of my mother's friends. Unfortunately he was what was then called 'backward', despite assurance that he was a 'Nice little boy really' he took advantage of such occasions to thump me. Any attempt at self-defence let alone retaliation was countered by tearful complaints bringing down upon my head severe recriminations. My fear of even the most harmless and amiable of simpletons has remained with me all my life. Later I had another disincentive to the enjoyment of birthdays, the payment of an endowment premium. My father had the foresight to take out a 'With profits' policy in my name which ensured that I had the wherewithal to buy a house by the time I was fifty. He paid the premiums whilst I was a child, but when I was 21 I took over, and a few days before each birthday the ominous reminder would arrive and I was required to fork out £10. The policy matured at double its face value but fell short of the price of a house, it barely funded a change of motorcycle.

Even the dullest and chilliest of the sporting excursions were preferable to being taken by my mother to 'her meetings' where ladies drank tea and I had to sit still and be quiet while they talked endlessly about grown-up things such as politics, which I assumed to be something to do with a parrot that had swallowed a clock. Invariably in one corner, hatted and shawled, sat an old lady of formidable appearance and quite unbelievable age to whom I was constantly and repeatedly enjoined to be polite and to say 'How do you do' nicely. It was many years later that I realised that this was Amy Dillwyn the legendary doyenne of local industry. The daughter of one of Swansea's formidable metallurgical dynasties had as a young woman suffered the death of both her fiancé and her father in quick succession. Her father left her with little but debt. As a well brought up Victorian girl, being unacquainted with much other than needlework and sketching, she took charge of her father's affairs, sold the much mortgaged estate, moved into a cottage where she lived in monastic austerity and set about turning his loss making zinc works into a profitable enterprise. It must have caused her some chagrin when the daughter of one of her staff having married a baronet became the chatelaine of the magnificent mansion where she had been brought up.

Fortunately when in Miss Dillwyn's company one was immune from that small boys' nightmare – being kissed by 'honorary aunties', the ugliest, smelliest and most repellent usually being the most insistent. More frequent and only marginally less objectionable, were the constant comments, 'Hasn't he grown?' I now sometimes wish I had had the cheek and the vocabulary to respond, 'Of course he's ----ing grown, that's what little boys do!'

2

Parents and Things

My mother was a small woman who surrounded herself with a quite awesome air of propriety, but was hard of hearing, very trying for those around her, but in one respect a boon to my father, since it enabled him to speak Welsh which to her was a serious no-no. Of more practical use was the fact that he could break wind in her company with impunity. Unfortunately he sometimes forgot that not all ladies were deaf, the resulting embarrassment frequently being compounded by his sotto-voce self-congratulatory critique of his performance. On the other hand my mother's oral flatulence was loud, prolonged and unashamed, belching in a fine Welkin-ringing, coloratura contralto. Far from considering it opprobrious she viewed 'Her Wind' as an affliction demanding sympathy.

My mother could be described as 'enjoying bad health' continually announcing her imminent demise and for decades she took out quarterly rather than annual subscriptions to Boot's library. Each summer, Christmas, New Year or any other annual event was always declared to be her last. When I took my fiancée to meet her she expressed regret that she would not see us married (she lived to see our Silver Wedding).

Periodically she would take to her bed and Nurse Ladd would be summoned. She was an impressive figure, tall and straight as a guardsman, clad in the nurses' appurtenances of cuffs, apron and table-cloth headdress, all so seriously starched as to impede movement. On arrival before even looking at her patient, she would greet me with a thunderous

'Have you BEEN today?'

Since she was such a firm believer in the curative powers of the enema and the suppository, it was wise to answer quickly and convincingly in the affirmative.

Whether or not under direct medical supervision, my mother would issue constant communiqués concerning her symptoms. A favourite response to anyone incautious enough to enquire as to how she was feeling was liable to be told that she was, 'knocked up', which if the enquirer was American caused some misunderstanding. Despite having a 'chest' and a 'digestion', she attributed ailments in others to weak-mindedness, and to admit, however indirectly, to any problem below the waist, was attributed to a wilful intent to disgust.

She knitted and embroidered and was almost as good a cook as she claimed to be and despite her somewhat bucolic background she was 'quite good' with say electricity and could change a plug or mend a fuse or oil the Hoover, tasks that were well outside my father's perception envelope. In addition, she used an electric sewing machine which was then real cutting-edge technology.

She also embraced photography using the standard amateurs tool the 5/- (25p) Kodak Box Brownie, determined to record every stage of my development. It is interesting to reflect how relatively expensive was such a pursuit. An 8-exposure roll film cost 1/2d (6p). The chemist charged 1/6d (7½p) for 'Developing & Printing,' returning 8 negatives and 8 6cm x 9cm prints in a bright yellow paper wallet. Thus each print including those with heads cut off, those that weren't straight, those where the child subject pulled a face. Those where the female subject claimed that 'it made her look old', (But you are old, aunty), those showing people with trees or telegraph poles growing out of their heads and those that did not 'come out' plus the extra shots one took to 'be on the safe side' cost 4d. At a time when a large loaf, warm and crusty fresh from the baker's oven and 10% larger than the present machine loaf could be had for 4½d (or half price for a 'yesterday's loaf'), photography was not for the short-pocketed. My father never took photographs; the concept of holding the camera level and steady would have been too much of a challenge.

My mother's background is still obscure. I know that her father kept the Post Office and (only) shop in West Dereham, a village in west Norfolk, an area that was inaccessible and isolated until the coming of the railway less than 40 years before she was born and was only rail-connected to the nearest town, Downham Market, a decade before her birth.

As a young woman she helped her parents in the shop. Since both her twin brother and a younger sister were also doing the same thing, it must have been crowded behind the counter. She did not get on with her mother, so when her father died in 1907 when she was 23, it is unsurprising that she 'Jumped ship'.

She initially went to Speyside possibly to relatives of her mother, and presumably to 'help out' (domestic service?). The 1911 census shows her as being back in West Dereham, but shortly after that she appears in Swansea as political secretary to the newly elected MP Alfred (later Sir Alfred) Mond, later to become the first Lord Melchett. This was an important post as since the rise of the Labour Party, Swansea was no longer a safe Liberal seat. Although Mond had business interests in the Swansea area, his main industrial activities were in the north of England, thus he would need a trustworthy person to 'Watch the shop' while he was absent from the constituency.

To be plucked from behind the counter of a village Post Office to fill this post seems extremely strange, the explanation for which I only deduced long after her death.

Anyway she stayed with Mond through marriage in 1917 and widowhood half a dozen years later, until he lost his seat in 1923. By which time she had achieved some prominence, being a consultee in the design of the then proposed 'Garden City' layout of the Townhill municipal housing estate. She was also more widely known, a 1915 invitation from Mrs Asquith to an 'At Home' at 10 Downing Street, survives.

Despite, following a hasty second marriage, having a baby (me) in July 1924, she seems to have assisted Sir Walter (later Viscount) Runciman win the Swansea West seat in October, since he presented her with a large silver salver inscribed with his thanks.

However to return to my cogent times, she seemed to be critical of almost every one apart from 'her women', that is to say, members of the local branch of the Women's National Liberal Association, (At whose meetings I was an enforced attendee) of which she was the permanent chairman, but for everyone outside of that organisation, save for possibly the more august type of academic, her distaste was indiscriminate. Workmen were lazy; servants were stupid, shop assistants insolent, teachers ignorant and nurses quite unspeakable. All shortcomings from bad breath to bad manners, and even plain bad luck, were ascribed to 'bad breeding'.

Her political views were equally sweeping. Conservatives were liars, Liberals were traitors (she was a National Liberal, quite a different thing apparently) and Socialists, or 'Bolshies' wanted this country to be like Russia – since everyone in Russia wore jolly fur hats and rode about in sleighs like Santa Claus, this seemed to me to be a commendable objective. She unreservedly admired Scottish people, so whether to love or to hate socialist Ramsay MacDonald was an ongoing dilemma.

However whether to love or to hate Lloyd George presented no quandary since whatever his other failings were, there was one that was unforgivable – he was Welsh.

Her worst strictures were reserved for 'servants'. Space precludes even a synopsis of their alleged shortcomings. Like everyone in our circle, we had a maid. Not a daygirl like the aspirational upstarts amongst those of the 'Mechanics Class', but a proper live-in. By today's standards these young women were paid a pittance, 15/- (75p) per week being the norm. However, many a man raised a family on little more than

£2, so at a time when women were paid at best three-quarters of a man's rate, and a maidservant had free food and lodging, the pay was far from exploitative. What could be so categorised were the conditions. A minimally furnished, unheated and ill-lit bedroom. (40 watt is quite enough; you don't want her reading and getting ideas). Baths once a week, the inside lavatory a no-go area, (except to clean it), two hours off on a Thursday afternoon and perhaps the whole afternoon on a Sunday (Don't give her time to get 'up to mischief'). This latter apparently tied in with that most inflexible of rules – No Followers. To such refugees from Rhondda or rural deprivation, Thursday afternoon off was crazy, since all the shops were shut. This mid-week half-day is now a distant memory but apart from the odd corner-shop desperate for every shred of trade the closure was total. The day actually varied from area to area, Llanelli was Tuesday but rural Carmarthenshire was Wednesday, all very confusing. On Sunday the trade embargo was almost universal, one could play cricket in High Street on a Sunday except that 'Street Games' were prohibited on a Sunday.

However to revert to domestic servants, presumably this custom of only giving them time off when the shops were shut discouraged them from demanding higher wages!

For maids a 'Uniform' of mock-lace cap and apron was *de rigueur*, these were provided, just as well, since cost apart she could never have bought it herself since she had no time off when the shops were open. Even in a small house there was plenty for the maid to do, two or three grates had to be cleaned out and fires laid and lit, coal-scuttles filled and the remains of yesterday's fires riddled to separate the ashes from reusable cinders. Meals had to be prepared and tables laid, dishes and clothes washed and everything ironed. There were no detergents or aerosols and washing machines little more than scientific novelties, installed mainly to prove that you had 'Araaved'. There would be a vacuum cleaner, but carpet squares left surrounds to be polished. The furniture had to be polished, 'Silver' as the cutlery was called, had to be polished, the brass ditto in fact everything had to be polished except the grates which had to be black-leaded, the steps scrubbed and the knives bath-bricked on a knife board. I recall a maid teaching me to spell my name in bath-brick on the knifeboard. Rugs had to be hung on the line and beaten with a sort of wickerwork paddle with the sort of dedication that I am told ladies in Soho apply to a similar task.

Every Monday was washday, the kitchen and scullery were full of steam from clothes and sheets being boiled to death, the dirt having been abraded away on a corrugated brass washboard and punished with a dolly (a sort of stool on a broomstick). As far as the end result was concerned modern washing powder makers could learn from the then demonstration of 'Whiter than white'.

Not of course that the maid would have been working all the time, when her chores were done she was free to relax on the kitchen chair, this 'job and finish' concession being of scant use since it would be perilously close to bedtime before the job was finished. Even so to guard against her 'slouching around all day' the kitchen chair was hard, upright and preferably wobbly.

It always seems paradoxical to me that despite a lack of unionisation, no calling in the course of the 20th century, saw pay and conditions improve as much as did domestic service.

Anyway the shortcomings of 'servants' were deplored at every tea table. Apparently they had to be continuously supervised, and almost everything they did had to be redone 'properly', anything breakable they broke, anything unbreakable they 'ruined'. One wonders why anyone should employ someone who apparently made such a negative contribution to the household – I believe it was largely as a token of rank. A servant proclaimed one's membership of the Middle-Class, albeit at junior level, whilst two signalled progress into the higher echelons peopled by socially elevated persons such as the Gas Manager. One had the impression that to have more than two bordered on vulgarity.

It must be realised that amongst urban, middle class south-walians it was fervently believed that if one was to 'get on' one had to eschew that peasant vernacular, the Welsh language, even to talk English with a 'Welshy' accent was unacceptable. It must be admitted that there was truth in this, since opportunities for success within Wales were few, there being many examples of Welsh people achieving an eminence in English cities which they could never have done in the Welsh countryside.

However my mother pursued this dogma with a Jesuitical fanaticism – Welsh people were idle, untrustworthy, ill bred, common – the pejorative list was endless. Her deafness made some of her English pronunciations quaint, but her mispronunciation of Welsh words was studied and pointed. To have known that in later life, I could correctly pronounce, accurately spell and had even visited, places such as Machynlleth, would have caused her genuine distress. Had she realised that I could get my tongue around Rhosllaner-chrugog without resorting to the English cop-out of 'Roast lamb and rhubarb' would probably have induced apoplexy. Having some inheritance expectations, I lived in fear that she might discover that I did actually have some acquaintance with the Welsh language. Fortunately she died before she could suffer the public disgrace of seeing a book in the Welsh language openly displayed with her son's name on the cover.

In fact she gradually took less and less interest in my doings, in her later years I am sure she did not know what I did for a living. She was aware that I travelled a good deal which to her meant that I did not have a 'proper job'. She even suspected me of associating with foreigners and attempting to speak their language, thus exposing myself to the risk of picking up their loose morals. Her only foreign excursion was a weekend to see the Dutch bulb fields, but that was Holland where everyone spoke English and were ruled by a Queen who did not allow her male subjects to 'do their business' in public as foreigners in other countries did.

Although I knew my mother for half a century, I never discovered her religious beliefs. I suspect that she was brought up as a Methodist, but she had definite Anglican leanings, not from any dogmatic basis but rather because she suspected that it was the church that the Almighty would have attended. She did not attend herself, because Anglican churches were part of the Church in Wales, which automatically made them suspect. Nevertheless she determinedly held shares in Vickers mainly because of their homophonic ecclesiastical aura.

We did not attend any place of worship, except occasionally Llanrhidian Church where 'Uncle Ben' (A distant cousin) ministered. I believe that she feared that if any penchant towards attendance at a place of worship was inculcated in me, I might finish up in my father's family's place Bethesda. It was Baptist, which was acceptable, but it was Welsh which placed it in the Hottentots' human sacrifice category. I do recall my father once being allowed to take me to Pantygwydr Baptist Church, but that was English which presumably made it OK. Oddly I do have a very early memory indeed of being in a chapel that can only have been Bethesda. It was crowded and there was a lot of singing. At one point everyone stood up (Halleluiah Chorus?) and I was lifted down from the pew to stand terrified amongst the Grown-up legs, I must have been very small as the hem of the skirt of the woman on my right kept hitting me in the face. Presumably my mother must have been ill or absent for me to have been there.

Since she was surrounded by Welsh people, let alone married to one, she was at odds with most of her acquaintances. Presumably, due to something from her past she was singularly vitriolic about nurses and

Aberystwyth. Apparently the former were described as tarts, although the comestible connection escaped me, the latter was, she alleged, full of thieves, giving a vision of a place populated by men in striped jerseys carrying sacks marked 'Swag'.

Actually she did make an exception for one thoroughly Welsh person – Mrs Hughes, presumably because her husband was a professor. He was in fact Professor Ernest Hughes a most charismatic man who spoke of historical figures as if they were the closest of acquaintances. Young though I was, he subliminally inculcated in me a love of and a respect for the past that has remained and flourished all my life.

The future we do not know, the present we do not understand, therefore we must derive our wisdom from the past.

3

The Times and the Manners

It is not easy even for those with personal experience of the time, to realise what the town was like 'Between the Wars'. For starters the era was not called that – having suffered the 'War to End All Wars', there wasn't going to be another one. Although 'The Great War' was a difficult concept for a child to grasp, a mere decade after its end there must have been many memories of hardship and bitter bereavement concealed by the thinnest of carapaces of cheerfulness. I was aware of people complaining about those who 'Did well out of the war.' In a coal-exporting town, there must have been some who did very well indeed. There was a rippling undercurrent of anti-German feeling (Although some who had spent time in France, professed anti-French feelings in equal measure!) The word German was widely used pejoratively for gimcrack or sub-standard goods. For instance, seeking the defective bulb in a string of fairy lights would be called 'Looking for the German'. British and Best, held sway and *Vorsprung durch Technik* was far into the future. For toys rather than using die-casting, Germany stuck to their traditional use of tinplate and those exported to Britain tended to be from the cheaper end of their ranges so were flimsy and had sharp edges, thus their trains could not compare with Hornby and definitely not with Basset-Lowke. In fact few goods of any kind were imported. Washing machines and refrigerators came from America, but they were so few as to be statistically insignificant, Ladies had their Paris fashions, but the actual gowns were run up in the likes of Leeds. Cameras were the exception, Germany dominated the top end of the market whilst the ubiquitous Kodak was of course American.

As far as cars were concerned a Mercedes Benz was much too upmarket for south Wales, and BMW were sold as Frazer-Nash BMWs to give a reassuringly upper-class hyphenated British flavour to the marque. Opel cars were fine and very keenly priced but despite being an American owned firm, could not overcome the German stigma. Other 'Johnny Foreigners' were also demonised as not being up to British standards. Citroen dodged that obstacle by assembling in Slough and the 'Big Yanks' such as Buicks and Dodges gained acceptance by passing themselves off as Canadian. Motorcycles were the same, there was a shop selling American Indians, but I cannot recall seeing one on the road. The idea of a Japanese motorcycle (or car for that matter) would have seemed as likely as a chocolate teapot.

Although times were hard and there were those who allegedly put halfpennies on the tram-tracks to convert them into pennies, Swansea with its tinplate trade and anthracite coal, fared better in the 1920s and 1930s than say the steam coal districts of the Rhondda.

In Swansea, Cardiff-envy was endemic. Cardiff was more populous than Swansea, it was a *de facto* (although not yet *de jure*) capital city, and there were more Cardiffs worldwide than Swanseas. Against this Swansea could point to the time scarcely beyond living memory when Cardiff was a village and Swansea was the metallurgical centre of the world. It was still a town of big numbers claiming more acres than Birmingham; over thirty railway stations five of them main line termini and five docks. Although coal tonnages were a fraction of the glory days, it was a major oil port and when it came to the export of tinplate, nowhere on the planet could even come near the Port of Swansea. In addition it was claimed that both its rugby and soccer teams were better than Cardiff's.

Of the score or so of Swansea cinemas, the Albert Hall with its chic café liked to be thought of as the height of sophistication, but adults yearned for the times when it had been host to great occasions. They reminisced about how the rafters rang to the rhetoric of the likes of Lloyd George and where Madam Patti gave some of her many farewell concerts. They would describe how Adelina Patti-Nicolini, the Baroness Söderstrom would arrive at the Midland station from her Craig y Nos eyrie via her special train. How she progressed through the town in an open carriage with a mounted escort of the Glamorgan Yeomanry. Police controlled the cheering crowds, no wonder the children confused her with Queen Victoria. No wonder they rued the hall's relegation to cinematographic status.

The 'Al' was soon outshone by the palatial purpose-built Plaza. Both were 'First run' establishments showing the latest releases and charged up to half a crown (12.5p), both had cafes, but the Plaza had the clincher –

an organ that rose all lit up to play 'selections' between the films. However when we were older we appreciated the unique advantage of the Albert Hall, the back row seats were double and the usherettes were allegedly less assiduous in shining their torches to ensure that there were two hands on every lap.

There were lesser establishments such as the Carlton, Castle and the Rialto and below them the likes of the Elysium and the Picture House. These lesser establishments changing programmes twice per week consisting of a 'big' picture and a 'supporting feature' with of course the Movietone or Pathé News.

The two big theatres were the Grand and the Empire, the former overhung by the august ghost of Madame Patti. One was only taken there on rare occasions when there was a 'suitable' play. The Empire was a Music Hall with twice-nightly variety performances which being 'vulgar', were barred to the young. Pantomime was allowed although it proved confusing. Peter Pan, Beanstalk Jack or whoever, were I was assured all ladies, similarly it was not apparently rude to look when the ugly sisters showed their bloomers because they were really gentlemen. All most puzzling but nevertheless an opening to put the inevitably evaded question – what was the difference between ladies and gentlemen? This difference would in due course provide a compelling reason for cinema going, although for the time being we tended to patronise just the YMCA and the Uplands where on Saturday mornings for a trifling few coppers there would be Cowboys and Indians to be cheered and booed respectively, no fear of having to sit though soppy love stories.

Despite avoiding the worst of the 1930s slump, things were still tight and in an effort to provide work and to accommodate the burgeoning ranks of municipal functionaries, a new Guildhall was built except that it was not a mere Guildhall but a Civic Centre, a celebration of the greatness of the town and its Councillors. It would soon demonstrate that corollary to Parkinson's Law that unlike work that expands to occupy the time allotted to it, public pen pushers expand to exceed whatever space is allotted to them.

Instead of the soaring pilasters and porticoes more usually associated with civic aspirations, it was of an uncompromising Cenotaph-like bland whiteness. An appropriate design key it was alleged, since nothing much went on inside it. Despite the size and the eye-watering cost of the 'Civic', it failed to displace the primacy of Swansea's most iconic edifice – that great monument to respectable expenditure, Ben Evans.

Occupying almost the whole of what is now 'Waterfall Square', it purveyed everything from a 'button to a bus' and having an 'Account at Ben's' carried as much social cachet as did membership of even the most prestigious of the four golf clubs. Its rival store David Evans on the other side of Temple Street was in emporia terms a tad less prestigious despite its curtilage embracing Lloyds Bank, whereas Ben's encompassed the Three Lamps, a slightly racy pub. Ben's put on fashion shows, the David Evans equivalent were mannequin parades – occasions that were apparently not at all respectable, since nothing stigmatised with a French-sounding name could be entirely above board. I recall it being whispered that a neighbour's daughter was a mannequin and hence 'No better than she ought to be' (whatever that meant).

For shoppers seeking a less sophisticated and more Welsh ambience there was Lewis Lewis, '*Lewis dwywaith*' (Lewis Twice). Like most of the big stores the young women staff lived on the premises and whilst Mr. Lewis was undoubtedly most solicitous of his employee's welfare, this did not run to curtaining the windows of their bedrooms. Apparently these were overlooked by the upper floor of an adjacent pub, access to which could allegedly be gained for a small fee.

There were other lesser department stores such as Edwards' and D. J. Meyler, the latter with a grand staircase that bifurcated at a mezzanine in the grandest palazzo style, from where Mr. Meyler could stand Doge-like, his eagle eye seeking imperfections in his vassals. All these Temples of Trade were patrolled with measured tread by immaculately suited men, tall as trees, straight as guardsmen – the shop walkers, (portrayed to perfection in *Are You Being Served* by Captain Peacock).

At 'Bens' one's purchase money was put into a sort of little canister inserted in a door in a pipe and with a swish disappeared, to shortly reappear with the change and the receipt. Much more exciting were other large stores that had a network of little overhead railways with terminations in each department. The money would be put into a little cup that the assistant reached up to attach to a carrier at the end of the track and then pulled on a sort of elastic catapult that would send the cup and carrier shrieking and swaying along the tracks until it was lost from sight and sound. Its return would be heralded by a screaming crescendo as it neared what we would call today supersonic speed, to alarmingly crash into the track's ending above the assistant's head. Incidentally in such establishments nothing was priced in even shillings. A pair of gloves would never be priced at 2/- but at 1/11¾d whilst a hat might be 3/11¾d, or in shop assistants' jargon, three, eleven, three. Despite so many transactions involving farthings, actual farthing coins were uncommon, so a packet of pins or some other trifling haberdashery item would be substituted in one's change.

All men wore suits, some even wore formal 'Morning suits', either way they were 3-piece suits, failure to wear a waistcoat being a serious sartorial shortcoming, The waistcoat had to match the rest of the suit, and be single breasted; it might be possible for a camel-hair waistcoat to be passed off as an eccentricity, but a double breasted waistcoat in any cloth was the mark of a cad. Suits were invariably black or extremely dark blue, which when bought became the 'best' for Sundays and formal occasions, its predecessor being relegated to 'second best' for work. Should an ash man happen to be a Deacon at one of the dressier chapels he might well empty your bins clad in black jacket, striped trousers and even possibly a wing collar. Obviously for office, shop work or 'business' a suit was essential, so should a man be seen in say a sports jacket (extensively vented and box-pleated to suggest he was a horseman), it was a proclamation that he was a possessor of a selection of garments. A brown suit served a similar purpose, and was a garment with which it was permissible to wear brown shoes. A blazer and slacks could be worn for yachting, on the bowling green or watching cricket, but for other sports a dedicated suit was a must. Golfing demanded a plus-four suit, mountaineering a climbing suit and a rural walk a tweed suit. Indeed the term suits was so ingrained that overalls were called boiler suits. Today's range of informal clothing was unknown. Sartorial stricture extended beyond suits, my father's starched stiff collars were no longer essential, a soft stud-attached collar (with cufflinks obviously) being acceptable. In the best circles to wear a collar-attached shirt with buttoned cuffs risked censure and to be without a tie except perhaps on the cricket field was seriously slovenly as was any attempt to hold up one's trousers with a belt.

The seriously wealthy bought their suits from tailors such as Barclay Owen or Snipper Bros and others, where in an ambience more of a consulting room than a shop, they could select a cloth from swatches and be measured and advised as to what was the currently fashionable cut and, steered away from such sartorial horrors as double-breasted waistcoats.

On a slightly lower scale were the outfitters such as Archie Jones, D. L. Davies, who supplied all clothing requirements other than perhaps, hats for which any man who 'was anybody' was measured and fitted at Dunn & Co. Although one saw pictures in the papers of national figures in top hats these were only seen locally at weddings and funerals, professional men tended to wear bowlers although these were being edged out by Homburgs with younger men moving into trilbies and 'Pork-pies'. Unless a man was very young or very rich, to wear a cloth cap was a badge of proletarian status or if worn back to front, a motorcyclist. Baseball caps even worn the right way round were unheard of.

University undergraduates went hatless and it was the custom of young yobs to copy them in the hope that they might be mistaken for students – a vain hope since the yobs were likely to be conspicuously better behaved. These apart, both men and women had to cover their heads at all times, even a drunk lying rag-clad and destitute in the gutter would not be parted from his hat. Men took them off indoors but women did not, even a bed-ridden woman would not receive a guest hatless.

The less discerning bought their suits at multiples like 'Monty' Burton's or the Fifty Shilling Tailors or even the Thirty Shilling Tailors where for £1.50 a made-to-measure could be produced in a time frame that Hong Kong could scarcely match today. The more staid and less sartorially adventurous citizens remained loyal to Hodges, where they would be greeted by name and discreet sympathy expressed if a waistline be found to have expanded.

The ladies had the biblically named, but actually thoroughly Welsh, Theophilus as well as Moriaty, Belmont, Evans Lassam and numerous smaller shops, where dresses were called 'gowns'. There was also plethora of specialist shops, tobacconists, stationers, bookshops, electrical shops, there was even Dickens who sold, repaired and even re-rolled umbrellas. There were also shops that sold unornamental ornaments – they were called gift shops.

However bestriding the upper-middle class trade was Sidney Heath (whose prices earned him the soubriquet, 'Sidney Thief'), his claim to clothe 'Gentlemen and their sons, ladies and their daughters' epitomised his market niche. It was said that the staff were reprimanded if caller left without buying, even if he had only come in to ask the way or the time. Many works and businesses fielded football teams, but Sidney Heath showed its distinction by turning out a cricket XI clad in immaculate whites (reputedly borrowed from stock) with an S H emblem on their caps.

At the other end of the spectrum were shops like The London Hosiery Company who could at a push supply a pair of trousers for 1/6 (7½p). Speaking of which no woman other than a horse rider or a dedicated sporting cyclist would appear in public in a bifurcated garment any more than she would be seen smoking in the street.

Small boys fortunate enough to escape the 'Sailor suit' tended to be dressed as 'little gentlemen' with hopefully nothing that could be construed as 'cissy', which would be at best social suicide at worst invite a serious thumping. I recall an occasion when visiting a school friend on a cold evening, his mother insisting that I accept the loan of a scarf to go home. To my horror I was forced to wear her daughter's High School scarf. Obviously as soon as I was out of sight I tore it off and hid it inside my coat, but I lived in fear that I had been seen and would be pilloried as a 'Cissy' for wearing a girls' garment. As for wearing an earring, a boy would be stoned to death on sight!

Pre-school girls wore what we might now call mini-skirts with matching knickers, those a little older wore dresses of a more demure length with underwear the colour, nature and even presence of which was the cause of much speculation, but of course never trousers.

In the then absence of charity shops, the lowest echelons of the clothing trade were occupied by 'Old clothes women'. Renowned for their discretion they would buy surplus garments from financially straitened households in say Sketty and sell them on in less privileged parts of the town.

4

Food, glorious Food

In the town itself as far as food was concerned, 'Company shops' – Liptons, Home and Colonial, Maypole (The Mape) predominated, but against this tide John Roberts of Waterloo Street resolutely stood out, although for really high class comestibles Taylor's held sway. A veritable Fortnum and Mason whose Wind Street threshold as Mr. Taylor made clear, it was a privilege to cross. Mr. Gale's High Street emporium was marginally less prestigious. So to maximise attraction he placed a coffee roaster in his window its fan-ducted pheromonic aromas filling the entire length of High Street from the station and via Castle Street and Castle Bailey Street, to Wind Street where they mingled with the hop-laden fumes of the brewery.

All except the smallest food shops had a provisions side and a grocery side. Generally males staffed the former, females the latter. The traditional strict dress code for male assistants had largely been abandoned but in some shops the ordinary assistants still wore their white aprons over their suits, the boss wore his under his jacket. The 'Prov' side was where the great red and silver bacon slicers stood where from gammons, backs and shoulders, rashers were effortlessly peeled off in chosen thickness, were deftly caught in a tasteful fan in a sheet of greaseproof paper held by the bacon hand or in the case of a favoured customer, by the manager himself. Likewise the carving of paper-thin slices from the bread-crumbed cooked ham. Lesser tasks such as slicing up with evil-looking garrotter' were the great round 40lb (18kg) cheeses wrapped in cloth (Cheesecloth) delivered to the shops in crates of two from Canada. Effetc Dutch cheeses and smelly French products were shunned. The scooping up of butter, either New Zealand in tapered wood 56lb (25kg) tubs, or Welsh butter, glistening with salt and beaten into submission with patterned bats was delegated to the lesser hands. Whether butter or cheese, the skilful assistant knew his job and his customers. If for instance half a pound (8 ounces, 227 g) of either was ordered, it would be cut or slapped with great ceremony and popped onto the scales. It invariably would be over and there would be an apologetic,

'Whoops sorry, is nine and a half ounces too much?'

A very skilled and experienced man could get away with up to 50% over.

The excitement of the grocery side was different – lots of smells from the sacks, bins and canisters of coffee, herbs, spices, cloves, currants, nutmegs and other mysterious exotica. Tea, sugar and flour came pre-packed, but many other things such as rice, tapioca, sago and lentils were scooped out of sacks to be meticulously weighed into blue bags carefully weighed and skilfully folded to secure the continents. The whole transaction arbitered by the big brass balance with its suspended pans and bright brass weights, which dominated the Grocery side.

Groceries included canned goods, especially those

Sunday teatime essentials Sardines and tinned peaches plus canned milk came in various guise. Corned beef and tinned salmon were available but they were both so cheap that to serve either to guests was to court social ostracism. Canned vegetables were not a big seller, but dried peas were a big item either weighed out from the sack or in cardboard drums that also contained a net bag and bicarbonate of soda tablet for soaking them overnight. Salt came in wrapped blocks like today's bread, which of course then was never wrapped.

Whilst the variety of foods was by modern standards limited, there was a plethora of brands and labels, national regional and local, the latter produced by the local wholesalers. Retailers brands were very rare except in the largest of the 'Company chains' and of course the Co-op, which branded everything. (Not that anyone we knew would be seen dead in a Co-op shop).

Whatever the shop the customer would expect to sit down while the requirements were assembled on the counter. The whole would be totalled in pencil on any scrap of paper. The assembled pile would either be loaded in the customer's curved basket or packed into a box for the boy to deliver. There was never any delivery charge. Actually some of our posher friends did not visit the shop at all, telephoning their requirements, very posh persons would not even telephone, but would expect the shop to send someone round (to the back door, of course), to take the weekly order.

Besides the grocers most other food was from specialists, fishmongers with their wares displayed, a thousand eyes staring accusingly at one from the Cold Slab as if blaming you for their misfortune. Bakers baked tin and sandwich loaves, milks, cottages and bakestones, they all baked in the early hours, one would be as loath to buy a 'yesterday's' loaf as a yesterday's newspaper. Dairies sold milk, cream and eggs. Welsh Produce shops unsurprisingly sold Welsh produce, pies, fat farm bacon and butter saltier than the bacon, plus laverbread that curious comestible regrettably reminiscent of the consequence of bovine diarrhoea, displayed in huge earthenware bowls. Poulterers sold poultry, what else? Greengrocers sold cabbages, 'colleys' and 'cukes', and pears, apples – both 'eaters' and 'cookers'. Almost nothing other than the Fyffe's bananas and the Jaffa oranges was imported. Without air freight and deep-freeze, fruit and vegetables were strictly seasonal and locally grown, Exotica such as Kiwi Fruits and Paw Paw were quite unknown while the likes of apples and pears (English of course) were prized for their taste rather than their colour. Potatoes had to be Gower or Pembrokeshire at a pinch, and tomatoes Jersey. Butchers and even pork butchers shops abounded. From a child's viewpoint even more interesting than the ice-cream parlours, the toyshops or the numerous sweet shops were the cake and pastry shops every one a cornucopia of custard slices, éclairs, chocolate boxes, almond boats (with rice-paper sails) all 2d each or seven for a shilling (5p).

Of course in the less posh areas there was a shop on almost every corner, often 'Parlour Shops' with no actual shop window, the front room used unconverted with reserve stock stacked in living rooms and on and under the stairs. The ultimate parlour shop was on the Townhill council housing estate where business was conducted in the fully furnished living room with goods on offer being piled on the table, chairs, settee, with the overflow in the passage and up the stairs. Since engaging in trade on council houses was a big no-no, the entire stock was taken upstairs to be hidden in the bedrooms when the rent-man was expected.

Similar enterprise was shown by the keeper of a shop in one of a row of tiny industrial dwellings. Additional trade was conducted from a pony and a two-wheeled cart. Out of business hours the cart was kept, upended in the communal yard alongside the communal toilet whilst the horse was kept in the kitchen.

Some of these shops were very small indeed catering for perhaps less that half a dozen families but supplementing their takings as 'Convenience stores' expecting at anything up to midnight calls of the 'An ounce of tea quick, the kettle's boiling', nature.

Many of these small shops were (probably from necessity) 'careful' with money. It is said that one, a chemist as it happened, would not use a bank since it would enable the 'girl clerks' to know his business. His suppliers' demands to be paid by cheque put him in something of a dilemma that was eventfully solved by using false name for banking purposes. Another would write the cheque sum in red ink and the payee and signature in black ink since he believed that this artifice would make forgery more difficult, there was another who had no cash register but kept his money in a drawer. Whenever a customer proffered a coin, he would bounce it on the counter (It was widely believed that forged coins would not bounce). He bounced the coin with one hand while the other he unlocked the under-counter draw for a split second to catch the bouncing coin. The florin-half crown trick was endemic amongst small traders. These coins worth 2/- (10p) and 2/6d (12½p) respectively were easily confused, so if a half crown was handed over for a small purchase, change from a florin might well be given. There was one greengrocer who would hand over the inevitable 'short change', and then if the customer's hand was not withdrawn the extra 6d piece would be reluctantly added. There was a tale of a shop kept by two maiden ladies where when a man offered coins he would be directed to put them into a slot in the counter where they fell into a bowl of disinfectant.

These independent shops survived because they gave credit, which the 'Company' shops did not. The more upmarket shops presented their bill at the end of each month and there was a certain type of customer who thought it smart to keep the tradesmen waiting and there were even tradesmen who thought it equally smart to be kept waiting. At the lower end of the scale people bought daily and settled (or failed to settle) on payday. Extended credit was the downfall of many grocers.

Bakers sometimes sold 'off the cart' but more usually made regular deliveries. Milk was delivered to the doorstep by horse and cart, in glass bottles but the traditional custom of filling the housewife's own jug from pint and half-pint measures still persisted. Either type of milkman would have been equally amazed to learn that the skimmed milk which they almost had to give away, was being sold at the same price as 'proper' milk.

One item that was rarely delivered was the weekday paper, although since the newsagent's shop would be closed, Sunday papers were hawked door to door. Tinkers with handcarts mended kettles and pans, while the knife grinder pushed an intriguing machine with a single bicycle-type wheel. This singular device would be inverted and the single wheel would form part of the foot-operated power train that turned the little grindstone, that with sparks and a tooth-on-edge shriek would do the sharpening.

One street trader happily absent from the streets was the ice-cream van. The concept of a vehicle filling the street with *Greeensleves* at a volume unattainable by the largest brass band was unthinkable. Ice cream was bought and eaten in an 'Ice cream Parlour'. Whilst some Italians brought ice cream around in a handcart, peripatetic purveying was largely confined to beach-type areas and was done from 'Stop me and Buy One' tricycles. Walls and Eldorado competed to sell you a 1d (.42p cornet), whilst Lyons was way upmarket with its 2d choc-ices. (When we became old enough to be acquainted with such matters, ruder boys would suggest that contraceptives might be sold as 'Buy me and stop one).

Gypsy women were frequent callers, invariably

carrying a baby in an enveloping shawl and a basket of clothes pegs. These pegs were made by securing two pieces of split osier with a little tinplate band. The bands were made from tinplate 'wasters' begged from a tin works. Fifty years or more after this practice ceased, a derisorily small order would still be scornfully called a 'Gypsy order'. Even if one did not buy pegs it was considered prudent to 'cross her palm with silver and allow ones fortune to be told if one was to escape an evil spell.

More pathetic were the bemedalled men, often disabled who called door-to-door selling collar studs, matches or similar trifles.

Apart from the specialist sweet shops, all the smaller corner shops stocked sweets, almost exclusively brilliantly hued boiled sweets in 4½ lb (2kg) glass jars. When these were on the counter within reach, there were tales of customers helping themselves to a sweet and if it proved not to their liking, replace it half-sucked. Biscuits came to the shop in the traditional biscuit tins to be weighed out as required. The makers supplied stands to be put in front of the counter, to carry two rows of tins invitingly tipped forward with their lids replaced by hinged glass covers. It was surprisingly easy for the more intelligent type of dog to flip the cover open with his nose. Thus wiser grocers put Cream Crackers, Breakfast Biscuits and similar doggy-distained varieties in the lower row keeping the more caninely desirable Custard Creams, Bourbon and the like in the less accessible upper row.

On the subject of dogs, absent from every inventory

was pet food. For dogs, butchers sold off cuts at 4d (about 1½p) per pound and there were packets of Spiller's biscuits ad Winalot meal. All the cat got was maybe the odd fish head given away by the fishmonger and anything it could catch. The idea of canned pet food being a major industry would have seemed as ridiculous as importing flowers. In any case flowers were only bought for weddings, funerals and by husbands in serious trouble.

The 'Company' shops had their own supply chain, but the independent shops were serviced by an army of commercial travellers who took their orders and (hopefully) collected payment for the previous order. The former was easy the latter less so. In fairness the small grocer's lot was precarious, squeezed by competition from the Co-op and the Company shops. In addition they mostly sold on credit so if customers failed to pay neither could the shopkeeper. Some indigence was less genuine and numerous and imaginative were the excuses for not paying. 'Just used my last cheque' (A used-up chequebook was kept to add veracity. 'All my financial stuff is with the accountant', 'I didn't think I would be here when you called, so I put a cheque in the post'. A variant of this was. 'Wasn't sure if you were coming so I was just going to post it', In this case a sealed envelope would be handed over, which when subsequently opened had the wrong date or even no cheque at all! Should the cheque be dishonoured, this was never of course due to a shortfall of funds but a 'Mistake by the bank'.

I heard in later life too many reminiscences of mature spinster groceresses cheerfully negotiating an extension of credit or perhaps a substantial discounts, on a sack of peas or lentils in the back-of-shop storeroom. These tales were too widespread to be entirely fictional.

These 'Reps' would never call 'Unadvised'. That is to say without having his intention to call notified by post via an 'Advice Card'.

Most travelled by public transport, a car, particularly a 'Company car' being the exception and then it would be a basic Austin Seven, a small Morris or a Ford Popular. The grander ones arrived by train and were met by a boy to carry their sample-cases – or even a car and driver. Some big firms insisted that within towns their travellers walked, it being the only way to ensure than every possible outlet was called upon. On the other hand the very grandest gentlemen, would travel by train between major towns and when the train stopped at intermediate stations would expect retailers to be on the platform ready to hand their orders and payments through the window of their (First Class) compartment.

The Welsh valleys offered a particular challenge, they had to travel to the top of the valley then come back down to repeat the exercise in the next valley. Often passenger trains were few but carried a brisk mineral traffic. Passengers on business were customarily allowed to travel in their brake vans but had to pay first class fares!

There was a tale that the two competing flour suppliers to the bakers of the Swansea Valley, by mutual agreement, did not venture further than Pontadawe, leaving all the up-valley bakers to come down to a Pontadawe pub to announce their requirements and hand over their cash. Apparently a new representative for one of the millers, not knowing of this arrangement visited all the up-valley bakers – and secured all the business, establishing a monopoly which his firm retained until private baking ended in the 1960s.

My father's four travellers were not in the exalted category of those from Bristol and beyond, nevertheless his head traveller the formidable John Thomas Richards (JTR) Deacon Emeritus of Tabernacl Chapel Morriston, was such an exalted figure that I recall him being the almost automatic choice to open fetes and adjudicate at musical contests in some of the communities he visited.

There was a strict hierarchy amongst travellers and just as say butlers' pecking order was decided by the peerage rank of their employers, so a traveller's social standing depended on the 'House' he represented. Those travelling 'in' provisions (Bacon, Butter Cheese etc) outranked those travelling 'in' groceries. Â man representing a national firm outranked one representing a local one. A grocery man tended to hold a rank inversely proportional to the number of lines he carried. Thus Shredded Wheat man with just the one line would have considered himself a cut above the Kellogg's who ran several. Thus a representative from a local wholesaler with hundreds of lines was, the likes of JTR apart, well down the pecking order. Status was also affected by the mode of transport, the man with a car was superior to the man on foot (unless the car had the firm's name on the side) and less than the man on foot was the man with a van, especially if he 'sold off the vehicle' Although in contrast with the car situation the size of vehicle inversely affected status, the men with small vans selling tea or yeast carried more kudos than the soft drinks, or fruit and vegetables salesmen with a lorry.

Travellers from out of town used 'Commercial Hotels' which would normally have a Commercial Room where in the evenings orders could be written up and next day's Advice Cards prepared (Usually if posted before 9.30 pm they would be delivered next morning) Such hotels would also have a Commercial Table in the dining room where travellers would take their dinners and suppers in fine style. The custom of appointing the doyen of those present to preside and vet newcomers as to their suitability to join the exalted gathering did not entirely die out until the 1960s.

5

Tradesmen and Tramcars

There was a time when the name of the shop showed the supposed origin of the goods sold there. The draper would be 'Manchester House', the ladies fashion shop 'Paris House', the hardware shop 'Birmingham House' and any shop wishing to weave an air of sophistication around its modest premises called it 'London House'. Regrettably by my time, Swansea retailers were much too pretentious to adopt this hick nomenclature. Even so there were plenty of shops selling less interesting things such as stuff you couldn't eat.

Overarching retail trade from food to funerals, via hardware and furniture, polishes, soap and clothing was the Co-op. Everything was branded in fact they were the pioneers of 'Retailers' Labels' they even for a time sold their own make of pedal cycles – motorbikes even, headquartered in their Heathfield Street behemoth, the Co-operative emporium. The 'Divvy was everything, there are apocryphal tales of women having begged a box for firewood would insisting that they be charged for it so a dividend would accrue from the transaction.

Co-op shops found in every district and every town and village were a series of independent societies, who would vie to pay the biggest dividend. Some of these went into double digit percentages and could only have been paid by overcharging, but since no dedicated co-operator would even window shop in non co-op premises, prices were not compared. Whilst the aspirationally intentioned would prefer to be seen entering a brothel than a Co-op shop, the Co-operative movement had solid support from persons of even the mildest left-wing leanings so enjoyed a customer base that today's' big supermarkets could well envy.

There was no partisan opprobrium attached to that other Swansea retail institution – The Market. Market was a confusing title, people talked about 'Being in the market' when they were clearly not. When I heard that the 'Market had fallen', I expected to find a pile of scarlet Ruabon brick, but the next time we went to town, but there it was its windowless perimeter walls standing Petra-like 'Rose red, half as old as time', still buttressed by butchers' shops on the inside of its glassed-over expanse. Gower folk peddled their cauliflowers and cockles wall to wall, plus of course laverbread. Nearby Portland Street was the lair of the Vanguard buses that brought in the Gower folk, I am just old enough to recall women carrying in baskets of cockles on their heads.

Around the Market were the shops catering for the Gower trade. Griffiths the ironmonger, where in a dark maze of agricultural requisites the most arcane item could be instantly dug out and a price quoted, to be immediately reduced by a few coppers with a conspiratorial cough that inferred that the customer was of more than ordinary status. Or, Smith the Boots, with its skeins of robust footwear hanging outside the Union Street shop, where whenever, following much testing and deliberation, a pair of brogues was purchased, a tin of polish or a duster would be slyly slipped into the box beside them. Plus of course the Market Café where apronned stallholders met to deplored the derisory prices that cabbages and carrots were fetching.

Just as universally patronised was Woolworth's (or Wool's worth, as it was often called). Although basically classless, the High Street Branch was, despite identical pricing and stocking, somehow considered less downmarket than the Oxford Street branch, possibly because its premises had once been the ultra-smart Criterion Hotel. Planned in the euphoria of the post-war boom, opened just as the slump began to bite. Both branches offered everything from a packet of nails to household items at either 3d (1.25p) or 6d (2.5p) the larger items being broken down into several 6d parts. Although the name was a by-word for shoddiness, the value was in fact good; if one paid 6d for something that was 1/- (5p) or more elsewhere one should not expect the best. Wherever one went in the country the layout of every branch was comfortingly familiar. Necessities like electrical goods and hardware were at the back, while at the front where they could tempt one were 'impulse buy' items such as sweets. These displayed in cornucopian quantities were mostly priced at 2d (less than 1p) per quarter pound (113g), half or a third the going rate for top brands. More expensive items were sold if they could be separated into component parts each priced at 6d.

Marks & Spencer had the same layout of island counters as Woolworth's and were regarded by some as 'Cheapjacks' but their limit price of 5/- (25p) took them into a different, substantially clothing based, market.

The girls were regarded (undoubtedly incorrectly) as being a cut above those at Woolworth's. To call them girls was in no way condescending since few married women worked, so the majority of employed females were what we now call teenagers.

Bestriding all trade was the 'Half-day.' A few of the more upmarket 'gown' shops endeavoured to show their sophistication by closing on Saturday afternoons. Butchers were shut on Mondays (A relic of the freezerless times when all meat was at most 24 hours old and there was no killing on a Sunday). The only afternoon in the week when a stranger could be sure of finding a shop open was Friday, since no one would curtail their opening hours on payday. However at the time, all these mores and manners belonged to the alien realms inhabited by grown-ups and so were outside my awareness.

What were more within our ken were the toy and model shops. There were a number selling everything from a celluloid windmill on a stick to a pedal-car, but since they sold dolls and dolls' accoutrements, they were not proper places in which a boy might be seen. Boys went to Dan Morgan's, which was basically a cycle shop, and whilst it did purvey fairy-cycles and child's tricycles, it was the official agent for Hornby and Meccano so was a compulsory stopping-off point particularly in pre-Christmas and pre-birthday times. Messrs Hornby's trains gave rise to a rigid two-class system – boys with 1ft radius layouts and those with 2ft radius. To admit to belonging to the former was to admit to the shame of living in a house too small to accommodate the larger track layout and that one was denied access to the coveted bogie rolling stock. The only way a one-footer could salvage some shreds of his reputation was by having an electric locomotive. I had to endure the shame of 1ft radius and wind-up propulsion. Later Dan Morgan's was able to add a jewel to its diadem by becoming the agent for FROG model aeroplanes, which while not true scale models were made of a waxed-card simulacrum of the monocoque construction that was beginning to be used for the latest military aircraft.

The town had peripheral districts, I was familiar with Uplands, Sketty and to a lesser extent Mumbles but most were only names on the front of trams and buses, some with giggle-making potential such as Tycoch and more obviously Cocket. In fact places such as Fforestfach, Landore, Cwmbrwla and a dozen more were almost self-contained villages, each with their own characteristic ambiance. At each of these enclaves were shops of every kind and when it came to Morriston the presence of a Woolworth's enabled their residents to survive indefinitely without venturing beyond Woodfield Street and probably there were folk in the Mumbles who spent a lifetime without leaving The Dunns. Not that they would have had any difficulty in leaving the Mumbles, they had The Train.

In my earliest recollections, the Mumbles Train was a steam hauled assortment of disparate rolling stock, the most exciting being the open sided 'Toast Racks', but all provided the opportunity of open air rides on the upper deck. I can remember the incredible wonder of steam being replaced by the sleek electric double-decker super-tramcars, veritable rail-bourn Concords of their day. Rutland Street to The Dunns in an unbelievable 19 minutes. At quiet times the cars ran singly, but were more usually double coupled and exceptionally triple-coupled. The seats were sybaritic blue leatherette, but like the trams had hinged backs so that one could face the prevailing direction of travel. Alternatively the backs of an adjacent pair could be re-arranged to provide a sociable foursome. The seating at each end upstairs was in a curved couch, bay window formation a place that was eagerly sought. A placard announced that there was seating for 103 persons but no mention was made of any limitation on the number standing, which unlike the buses was allowed in the 'Upper Saloon' as it was tastefully called, enabling per-car numbers to approach 300. Once heard never forgotten was the scrape of the track, the click of the rail joints and the note of the Klaxon and most of all, the 'fwiiiishh' of the pneumatic doors. And there was the smell – that uniquely pungent electric-train smell.

Unlike the Mumbles Train 'Jet set', ordinary folk had to catch the tram, a rattling, shaking poor relation of the swish Mumbles trains, whose wheels banshee-shrieked as they suffered the track's twists, nevertheless they made a fascinating subject for study by small boys.

Each tram route had its distinctive cars. Possessing a status inferior only to Mumbles, Sketty folk travelled in the loftiest of double deckers if their designation was High Street Station and slightly racier models if their destination was The Docks. At the Albert Hall, these latter instead of going straight on, relied on a points boy to direct them down Cradock Street and Union Street to ess-bend past the flame-lit cavern of the shoeing-smith's forge, through Wassail Square with flanges screaming and on to their Fisher Street terminus.

Slightly less smart was the Brynmill route, which ran along Bryn Road and Oxford Street turning at Ben Evans' with again much protest from the wheel-flanges, towards its Wind Street terminus. The St Helen's tram ran along St Helen's road from College Street via what is now the Kingsway to the Slip, where on bank holidays and sunny summer Sundays hordes would pour across the Slip Bridge to the sands and during the week, clerks surreptitiously slipping off work to watch the cricket.

The Crewe/Clapham Junction of trams was contradictingly called Lower High Street a multi-terminus where trams lurked like birds assembling for migration, awaiting their turn to depart for such exotic destinations as Cwmbrwla, Brynhyfryd or Ynsforgan. Not far from this congregation was the Wind Street termination of the Port Tennant trams, squat even by single-decker standards to limbo-dance their way under the Fabian's Way Bridge near Weaver's.

Tramless outposts such as Cockett and Tycoch had buses, not the mighty Sauer Alpine vehicles that ascended from base camp in Trinity Place to the stratospheric heights of Townhill, but effete AEC double-deckers. For those pushing west of Sketty through the leafy lanes of Derwen Fawr, there were Leylands, from the front seats of which the driver could be closely observed so that one's fare included the acquisition of a modicum of driving expertise. As I recall the clutch and brake pedals were respectively stamped C & B, which presumably was to cater for a forgetful but reasonably literate driver.

Features of the suburbs were the delivery vans some still horse-drawn. All milk was delivered and most bread, as were meat and groceries, although the latter more often arrived by errand boy's bicycle. Ben Evans, Sidney Heath etc had vans, which raise the status of any house to which they delivered. There were also what we would now call mobile shops selling meat, fish or farm produce. In some areas carts or motor vans carried a selection of clothes and household drapery items, which would be sold on credit. These Credit Drapers were the descendants of the, Tallymen, Scotch Drapers, Chapmen or Packmen, who existed from at least the 17th century and informally known as 'Johnny Fortnights'.

Pride of place of these peripatetic purveyors was occupied by the lamp oil van. This latter sold buckets and brushes but its main trade was paraffin dispensed from a brass tap at the back, for which despite the urban near-universal availability of gas and electricity, there was sufficient residual distrust of both fuels to cause oil to be still widely used for light and some cooking. Lamp oil was apparently good business, certainly one paraffin peddler was able to send his son to a fee paying school, where he described his father as a 'Director of an oil company'. The lad tended to be evasive if questioned as to whether it was Shell or BP that his father directed.

Heating was by coal, carried in from a lorry in 1cwt

(50kg) sacks. Many bought single sacks, but it was quite usual to take 5, 10 or even 20 sacks. I recall one boy telling me how for as long as he could remember, it was the job of him and his brother to sweep out the coalhouse ready for when his coal merchant uncle delivered the usual 20 sacks. Eventually the uncle retired and they had to buy from a stranger therefore a strict tally was kept of the number of sacks being brought in. When this new coalman presented his bill he was told in no uncertain terms that only 19 had been delivered. The coalman pointed out that only 19 had been charged for since it was impossible to get 20 into the coalhouse.

As regards our street, one must be quite clear that unlike neighbouring thoroughfares the presence of a few trees enabled it to be called an avenue. Handy for the tram stop, the park and the allotments but it suffered from a crisis of locality, it bordered but could not be classed with posh Sketty and was perilously adjacent to the much looked down upon Brynmill. Closeness to the shops of Uplands, was a boon but that place and its pub was regarded as the resort of students and other scallywags. The nature of the housing added to the confusion Bisected by a cross street the steep avenue consisted of four distinct and very disparate blocks – what one would now call 'socially mixed'. On our side, the lower end comprised two pairs of semis. Our counterpart house was occupied by the owner of a typewriter shop whilst the other pair were respectively occupied by an ex Cape Horner harbour pilot and an elderly headmaster. Good solid stuff especially as the schoolmaster headed the prestigious Sketty Primary School. The picture of suburban respectability was somewhat marred by the pilot's grown up daughter who allegedly 'showed her legs in fashion parades', whilst for the three daughters of the typewriter man a 'bad end' was predicted since they were 'out until all hours with young men with cars'. Whilst car ownership was a badge of solid achievement amongst the middle-aged, in a young man it indicated that he had 'too much money', was in the motor trade or was a commercial traveller, categories along with the wearing of patterned pullovers or suede shoes made a young man 'unsuitable'.

Beyond the crossroad was a block of three commodious houses and a large detached property so was definitely nudging the Sketty bracket, while opposite them stood a near-mansion that confirmed the quasi-Sketty classification. We at the lower end might have basked in this aura of gentility had the entire opposite side of our end not been packed with a terrace of some score of almost Brynmill type homes. The occupants were doubtless worthy enough folk but since their political affiliations were suspect (One was known to be definitely a member of the Labour Party) we had little to do with them. Our house was a linoleum-floored kitchen with a black-leaded range, huge and with an appetite for coal to match, where cooking was done and formed a base for the maid. There was also the concrete-floored back kitchen where clothes and crockery were washed which had a gas stove used annually to steam the Christmas puddings. Most important was the larder, a narrow, lavatory-sized room whose massive slate cooling slab was backed-up by extensive wooden shelving. The ground floor was completed with two rooms, one to use and one to never use. Despite never being gastronomically employed the latter was called the Dining Room, the former in deference to my father's compulsive book-buying propensity was called the Library. Upstairs there were three rooms serving parents, maid and myself. There was a small aptly named Box room into which I was squeezed when my room was commandeered by Granny.

There were shops reasonably adjacent forming sort of outstations of Uplands – Davies, the squeaky voiced grocer pontificating on the issues of the day, Palmer the obsequious greengrocer, East the butcher, Rees the dairy plus of course A.E.Trick whose speciality was 'Letter biscuits', tiny slightly sweet biscuits in the form of letters of the alphabet which enabled a simultaneous assuaging of hunger and of illiteracy. The aim was to achieve by selective consumption and by judicious swapping one example of each of the twenty-six. The difficulty was that there was a dearth of the more substantial W's and a surfeit of the mingy I's, which were scarcely worth eating and useless as swaps. Actually entering his premises was discouraged because of his alleged Communist connections and his presumably agitprop clientele.

In the Uplands itself, trade revolved around Wayne's a food emporium where four middle-aged brothers hastened to do their father's bidding, with Phillips' next door vying for their trade, Green's, sweets and ice cream, Charlie Evans' the paper shop, Eynon's and Reed's battling for the bread and cake trade. Davies the posh fishmonger ('Heddick Medum?'), Miss Clement the fruitereress, Russell the Meat, C K Andrews 'Official Agents for Morris Motorcars', dispensing petrol from over-pavement gantries, Dixey the optician and the staid mahogany fittings of J T Davies; pharmacy competed with the somewhat slicker Boots for pills, potions and prescriptions, Whites sold shoes whilst an anonymous bewiskered man redolent of leather mended them amongst the whirr and slap of machine-belting. The opprobrium of the pub was counterbalanced by the respectability of the 3 or 4 banks. There was a hardware shop, a cinema and above all and of prime importance was Bennett's the Post Office not from any communicational possibilities but because tucked away in a glassed-in yard was a toy department, which a boy that had been very very good was allowed to enter.

6

Commerce

With a shop on so many suburban corner, Swansea's dozen or more wholesaler grocers battled for their business, they battled each other and with the interlopers from Cardiff such as William Powell whose fire-engine red Dennis behemoths lumbered in convoy with the understated greys of the sleek vans of the Danish Bacon Company. Impressive though these invasive fleets were, they were upstaged by the great noisy, smelly, yellow' steam lorries of David Jones. Locally based but whose Liverpool origin gave them a whiff of superiority that overlaid the choking fumes of their chimneys. David Jones' big brand was 'Golden Stream' tea that more vulgar youths said was the consequence of drinking it. Although my father's firm was not noticeably successful, his brand 'Investa' was sufficiently confusable with *Isvestia*, a Soviet newspaper much cited in the left-wing press, to give him a competitive edge among the more Lenin-leaning type of grocer. Likewise Harold Leigh's brand 'Kardov' was probably sufficiently Russian sounding to have a similar effect.

The wholesalers' vehicles were not the only comestible carriers, there were the scarlet Trojan vans of Brooke Bond Tea and the more restrained black and blue of the Morris-Commercial Lyons Tea vans, and there were the vehicles of the yeast peddlers and others struggling to put enough pennies together to make a shilling. There were the 'Pop' merchants' lorries delivering their bottles of luridly coloured, carbonated water copiously sweetened to meet juvenile tastes. At the upper end of this market was Bowen's, whose 'Big Four' (four flagons, each of a different colour in a wooden crate) were delivered weekly to the more affluent homes, but the mass market was met by Emanuel Thomas whose 'ET' brand was said to produce the maximum belches per bottle. The non-teetotal beverages were delivered by mighty men driving mighty horses, drawing mighty drays. In the pavement outside the pubs were steel flaps that gave access to the cellar enabling huge wooden barrels to be lowered by ropes down slides into the depths beneath. One member of the delivery team was stationed below to steady the descending barrels, a task that allegedly afforded a unique view of passing females.

Almost every building was heated by coal. The myriad grates, stoves, furnaces or whatever produced ashes which were sieved and resieved for reuse, just the dust being discarded to be collected by the horse-drawn Corporation dust carts, so-called because this dust was almost the only household refuse. There was no plastic wrapping and paper was used for fire lighting. Food scraps went on the garden; bones went first to the dog then to the rag and bone man who might well also take the food cans and bottles. Today we call it 'Re-cycling' then we just called it good household management.

The other major users of horses were the railways but to the chagrin of gardeners but the delight of small boys the G.W.R. replaced their live horses with Scammell

'Mechanical Horses'. These not entirely successful vehicles were a sort of miniature Artic having a 3-wheeled tug that had a remarkably tight turning-circle. The L.M.S kept their horses until the 1950s.

Handcarts were a feature of the streets, two wheeled, smartly painted and lettered with the proprietor's name and trade, plumber, decorator or whatever. If they were used by a painter or window cleaner, ladders rendered the Tee drawbar inaccessible, so the owner had to push and guide by the overhanging ladder.

The most exciting on-street show was the tarring. There would be a black sulphurous stinking, wheeled tar boiler, emitting evil smoke from its chimney. There would be two men with cloths over their faces like wild-west villains, one turning a crank on the tar-boiler to pump molten tar to his companion's spray-lance. When an appropriate area of the road surface had been covered, they would wield shovels to carefully scatter chipping. When this operation was complete, the mighty steam roller that had been sultrily hissing to await its cue to chuff back and fore crushing the chippings into submission. Seeing this was a rare treat since road so treated far outlasted those treated by modern 'carpet layering' machines.

Just as exciting and fortunately almost as rare was the sight of a fire engine. The gleaming brasswork that complemented the stark scarlet was matched by the shining brass helmets of the firemen who were not shut in purdah as they are in today's vehicles but sat in proud display on the outside. There were none of today's banshee wails, nor were there the anaemic ting-a-ling of the police car and ambulance bells, but the hearty clang of the great brass bell vigorously pealed by the driver's companion.

There was of course no long-distance road haulage; a 16 mph limit on solid-tyred lorries and 20 mph if on 'blow-up' tyres limited their radius. In the near non-existence of truckers' accommodation, if an overnight stop was called for in the absence of an enclosed cab, the driver and his mate might well sleep under their vehicle. Therefore most goods came by rail but quite a lot came by sea. Coast Lines brought canned goods and sugar from Liverpool and the Rotterdam-based 'Stroom' ships brought Continental goodies. Although this meant that like anyone in the food business on anything like a scale had to send their lorries into the docks to obtain supplies from what was regarded as alien territory.

My father like other 'Townsmen' regarded 'Docksmen' as an extra terrestrial species engaged in such arcane callings as 'coal' or 'shipping', but the division was not so much a matter of occupation as of location. If one's place of work was beyond the 'Checkpoint Charlie' of Wind Street Bridge, one was automatically a Docksman, regardless of your job or profession. The segregation was absolute and my eventual announcement that I intended to marry the daughter of a Docksman attracted not a little opprobrium. Thankfully my father did not live to witness the disgrace of my becoming in effect a Docksman myself.

Whilst like my future self, few, very few, Docksmen

were seafarers. Some might affect a nautical gait purely on the basis of an occasional Sunday paddle steamer trip to the Illfracombe bars; mostly the maritime connection was administering the export of coal and tinplate, and the brokering, chartering, or owning of ships.

Of course the glory days of the myriad coal tips being busy day and night, fed by five separate railways were over, but the collective memory was still vivid. There were many who claimed to recall the barques bringing copper ore from Valparaiso ('so many in the North Dock you could walk across them') and, indeed some genuinely did belong to that nobility of the dockland – the Cape Horners. They were men who had faced the shrieking, unforgiving winds of the Southern Ocean in tall ships. Men who, clinging to a lofty spar, had reefed main t'gallants stiff with ice, whilst the unrelenting scourge of torn canvas and flaying ropes threatened to dislodge their numb hands' grasp sending them to an instant death on deck or near instant death in the freezing quasi-Antarctic waters. When I was first made aware of these men I was too young to appreciate their heroism but realised they were somehow special and I should stand a little straighter in their presence.

The Docksmen had their own cafes and bars where deals could be struck and the passing of the good old days mourned. Some such establishments might be geographically in the Town area but they remained Docksmen's sovereign territory, like embassies in a foreign land. The bank managers frequented such places; presumably because everyone connected with shipping was in hock to them.

A sort of neutral frontier post was the Metropole hotel, where the upper echelons of Dock and Town could mingle. Situated at the bottom of Wind Street, it was handy for the docksmen and for the Coal Exchange, and not too far from the commercial premises of the town. Almost backing onto it was the Metal Exchange whose levers of power had worldwide influence and whose members and their minions could covertly access the Metropole bar via a discreet door in Salubrious Passage. Big deals were done in the Metropole Grill Room dominated by its shining, flame-licked silver grill. Lesser transactions were conducted in the bar; sea captains could take a drink with shipping agents or be libatiously solicited by chandlers or ship-repairers or, so it was said, ply fur-coated but allegedly lingerie-lacking ladies with port and lemons whilst negotiating transactions of a different kind.

Firmly in landsman's territory adjacent to High Street Station were the Great Western and the Mackworth hotels, the former was the resort of commercial travellers who allegedly put the washbasins to unintended use, but the latter was a hostelry of some standing where gentlemen lunched and dined and persons of import from Bristol or London lodged. The Mackworth was only yards from the station taxi rank so that if that destination was given to a cabbie, the fare risked having a tour of the town before being deposited at the hotel's glazed canopy. On the other hand if directions were sought from a passer-by the visitor might well be advised to take the underground only to find that the steps only led down to a gentlemen's convenience.

Further down High Street was The Bush, an inn with proud coaching antecedents whose *porte cochier* must have sheltered many a couple, respectively in breeches or crinoline arriving to take the invigorating airs at what was once a fashionable resort. Regrettably its name induced sniggers in the coarser type of youth.

Unlike the Metropole these three hotels would survive the Nazi aerial onslaughts, although the Mackworth with its exciting arcade shops would eventually succumb to the developer's wrecker ball.

This of course was High Street, which grown ups were liable to claim 'Wasn't High Street any more', which since the signs all still said High Street was a difficult concept for a small person to grasp. It still had some reasonably posh shops, but possibly none posher than H. A. Chapman the 'Photographic Artist' from whose window generations of the 'Crachach' (Snobs) stiffly stared, posed in front of the same Victorian whatnot. Rather towards the other end of the spectrum was the 'Adam & Eve', a pub with a fine painted sign, depicting the eponymous pair naked, but with their rude bits infuriatingly embroiled in foliage.

In Castle Street equidistant between the Mac and the Met was R.E. Jones' Restaurant the last remnant of the once nationwide R.E. Jones catering-to-cars commercial empire, under whose swishing ceiling fans a deal could be struck whilst a steak was demolished. Adjacently, lesser persons of fashion might sip coffee at the Kardomah, where my mother would take me for a lemonade and a Jacob's Club biscuit, provided she could find a table well removed from 'those vulgar young men' as she called Dylan Thomas and his acolytic court.

For more informal refreshment there were the cafes, mostly with exotic names such as Rossi, Rabaiotti, Greco or Cascarini. There, huge silver Gaggia geysers which with great swiiissshes and clouds of steam dispensed tea or coffee or steamed meat pies into soggy submission, where ice cream or Welsh rarebit or chips with anything was served on tile-topped tables. It remains a blight on the town that the premises of such upstanding people would be trashed when Mussolini entered the war on Hitler's side.

For more serious gastronomy than café fare there was Woolworths above their High Street shop, not a restaurant nor a café but a cafeteria where one pushed a tray along a chrome runway making one's selections as one passed, in a manner then novel but now all too familiar.

Whilst I have been unable to establish a causal connection, the great south Wales bonanza ended with my birth. The demand for both coal and ships to carry it had remained ahead of supply from the late 19th century, creating a boom. In the Great War (as they called it until we had another necessitating the numbers 1 & 2). Germany occupied the French coalfields, turning the boom into a bonanza. With the war's end in 1918, this bonanza had become a frenzy. Then suddenly, the French had plenty of coal, new ships burned oil, prices collapsed, coal piled up, the whole Cornucopia of Commerce came crashing down.

Indeed by the 1930s when my recollections gel,

strikes had further eroded coal export markets, causing a colliery depression that dominated every aspect of trade, bringing tough times to all but none more so than ship owners. With scrap prices collapsed they could not even give their vessels away to ship breakers. I recall as a child hearing of a vessel being aground in the Wash. This was puzzling enough – why should a ship be in the laundry? But even more so were the congratulations showered on the owner, coupled with the expressions of hope that it would not be found possible to refloat it.

Although that alien dockland territory was shrouded in enigma, there was no escaping its presence. The clank of shunting, the puff of engines, the groaning of cranes, the clatter of coal tumbling down the hoists and the sirens of ships pervaded the whole town. But more than that, Weaver's Hooter ruled the town. From its dockside reinforced concrete monolith of a flourmill it not only punctuated town life, but it also signalled every celebration and commemoration. It joyfully welcomed the New Year and each November 11th it prompted the bugler on the steps of the Daily Post to sound the Last Post bringing the town to a standstill. For two minutes all traffic stopped, tram drivers and conductors stepped down to join bareheaded pedestrians stiffly standing, motionless policemen held the salute and all sound both from town and docks ceased until Reveille echoed from Ben Evans' walls.

There were other reminders of the maritime connection. Lascar seamen, Indian-filing up Wind Street behind the Serang, their possessions in big, round toffee tins. Outfitters proximate to the docks displayed officers' caps and be-braided tunics and, smelling of tarred rope and exotic spices, were the chandlers. The doyen of these latter was Ove Lohmann; a reassuringly rotund and dignified figure as became a Knight of the Danish Court but who, if the committing of Grievous Bodily Harm to the English language had been an indictable offence, would have faced long periods of incarceration. However even the Lohmann presence was eclipsed by Lars Knudsen, whose cavernous emporium stocked every requisite any seafarer might require from a marlinspike to a 'Donkey's breakfast' (straw mattress), seemed to epitomise the Viking Swyne from whom Swansea allegedly derives it name.

Even these characters were outdone if not in stature, but certainly in girth, and gravitas, by Pierre Le Bars. He was the French Consul, but his 'day job' was representing a firm of French coal importers. A lesser man might have been called an Agent, but Monsieur Le Bars (never, Heaven forbid. Pierre) was more a Legate in the medieval mould. The Doges of Venice, the Medici's of Florence or indeed a Borgia, would have been proud to have such a man represent them at an Imperial court.

Although it did not impinge on my awareness at the time, Swansea despite a strong theatrical tradition had few females claiming thespian connection, contrasting with neighbouring Llanelli (or Llanelly as it was called in those days), where, particularly in streets adjacent to the docks and despite a dearth of stage job opportunities, 'actresses' abounded. This lack of loose ladies and indeed, by seaport standards, a paucity of pubs, was probably due less to chapel-imposed rectitude than the fact that most ships were locally crewed. Therefore sailors were liable to be dispossessed of their voyage pay at the quayside by umbrella-brandishing wives. Thus sober shore-time comfort was derived from families and their 'monkey puzzle' tree, sprung from the *Araucaria araucana* seed souviniered from Santiago in their far-off cabin boy days.

The local paper (or papers – there were two then) reporting a townsman's death would give fulsome details of occupation and church or chapel affiliations as well as manifold good works but when the death of someone of maritime inclination was reported it would be just a bald 'Death of docksman.' Yet there was one man who seemed to bestride the Town/Dock divide with ease – W.A, (or as he later became, Sir William A) Jenkins, combined being a self-made ship owner with the pervasion of every aspect of town life. No meeting could be chaired, no bazaar opened, no appeal launched, no public event held, without a speech from him. He was imposing, authoritative and carried weight in every sense. Some men manage all three without pomposity, but regrettably that skill eluded 'WA'.

The town was not of course bipedal, it was tripedal resting not on just Docks and Town, but also more importantly, on Industry. With nine tinplate works within its boundaries, it had 50% more than the self-proclaimed 'Tinopolis' of Llanelli. There were almost a score more tinplate works in the immediate locality with a plethora of steel, zinc and copper establishments, not to speak of collieries without number. Whichever way you looked at it Industry out-topped Town and Docks combined yet this very engine-room of the town had little impact on my childish perception. Partly this was due to Swansea's 'village' nature, our 'village' being non-industrial and partly because 'getting one's hands dirty' was so reprehensible even when done vicariously as a manager. Probably it was chiefly a throwback to when Swansea promoted itself as a Beau Nashish watering place, and 'manufactories' and any premises likely to emit smoke or smell was banished to extra-mural locations and like bodily functions not a fit subject for polite mention.

7

Town & Gown

Although thoroughly Anglicised there was sufficient residual Welshness in Swansea for there to be little class distinction based on background, occupation or wealth, what snobbery that did exist was district based. 'West of the river' was superior to 'East of the river', Sketty was, or thought it was, better than Uplands, and both considered themselves a cut above Brynmill and so on, finishing with Morriston people who knew they were a class above everyone else.

Mumbles had a unique an unassailable cachet, partly because it carried the last vestiges of Swansea's aspirations to be a fashionable seaside resort, but mainly because its people came to town by train. This was not an ordinary train like the LMS from Killay or Dunvant, or the Midland from Glais and certainly not the GWR 'Low level' from Morriston or Landore, but The Mumbles Train. Just as City financiers arriving by the Brighton Belle would consider themselves a breed apart from those commuting by ordinary train, so 'Mumbles Trainers' were a sort of elite. Thus a labourer in a cottage in the Mumbles would consider say, a Chartered Accountant his social inferior if the latter lived in Tycoch.

There was no 'racism', there was only one person in the town of African origin, but he wasn't a Negro and certainly not a 'nigger' – he was Darkie Davies. Notable not for his skin colour, but for his immaculate brown suit, brown overcoat and brown bowler hat. Elegance and countenance apart, he stood out from the crowd since one leg was permanently bent so that he had to walk with one foot on the kerb and the other in the gutter, whilst following his profession of 'bookie's runner'.

Since there were no betting shops such persons performed a valuable service. Then as now the placing of bets in the street was illegal, therefore periodic apprehension and fining was a hazard of the calling, which Darkie accepted as an unavoidable business overhead, devoid of any pigmentational prejudice.

Any English/Welsh linguistic confrontation had generally yet to arrive, but the religious apartheid was absolute. Not Catholic versus Protestant or even Church versus Chapel or Christian versus Moslem, (there weren't any of the latter); the main confrontations were within denominations.

The Anglicans generally kept to their parishes, except that certain churches were more fashionable than others but when it came to some of the 'free' churches as they were then called, matters tended to be considerably more complex. Capel Gomer (Welsh Baptist) would be more likely to invite the Pope to preach than welcome any member of Bethesda (also Welsh Baptist). The Wesleyan Methodists, Calvinistic Methodists and Congregationalists, both English and Welsh each tended to have two establishments apiece; one to attend and the other never to set foot in. Thus discounting the lesser denominations such as Unitarian, Seventh Day

Adventists or Christian Scientist, the four main non-conformist sects could require some 16 places of worship. Magnificent erections they were, Athens had just one Parthenon, Ephesus one temple, but in Swansea pillared, pilastered, portioned and pedimented sacred edifices glared at each other across almost every street, not to speak of the soaring Grampian-like pinnacles of the Scottish Presbyterian church. Besides St Mary's church recently rebuilt, an exercise, which shortly would have to be repeated, there was a plethora of other churches defying the dissenting hordes. Further from the urban epicentre the structures were grander, in the west churches that were majestic manifestations of the Gothic Revival and in the industrial east and north vast chapels, cathedrals of nonconformity, both kinds built by magnates anxious to secure their place in the Hereafter with tickets of stone and stained glass.

It is paradoxical to be talking about religious observances vis a vis my father, since having attended chapel three times every Sunday as a boy, by the time he reached adulthood he considered that he had completed his lifetime quota.

Whether he feared the hereafter, I do not know, in any case he was preoccupied with more immediate sources of terror, his brother, his sister and above all his wife. He avoided them all by going to 'meetings' whatever those were, although they were apparently very important. Some of the most demanding seemed to be the Chamber of Trade and the Chamber of Commerce. The purpose of these was a mystery to me since 'chamber' had but one meaning.

My early education was private so I escaped incarceration in one or other of the primary schools such as St, Thomas or Brynmill, that still tower above their surrounding streets like municipal cathedrals, or even Terrace Road embedded into the hillside so that however many storeys you ascend, you are still on the ground floor, with an ambience so Tibetan that the absence of Sherpas is disconcerting.

Instead I started at a kindergarten (a posh term for a Dame School) where I played in the school band. The brighter pupils played the tambourine, the less gifted such as myself formed the triangle section. One seriously fat girl found both instruments beyond her so she was allowed to conduct, it being understood that we were to ignore her frenzied arm waving and respond to the gestures of the mistress standing behind her. I also learned the wisdom of keeping my head below the parapet so to speak. It happened when the key to the back door could not be found. I heard the whisper that it was in the bucket under the sink so when the headmistress demanded to know where it was, I in my wish to please told her where it was. Not only did the information fail to please her since she assumed that it was I who had put it there, furthermore I was thumped by my classmates for 'snitching'. Oddly, I made more life-long friendships here than at any subsequent incarcerations.

My next school was a 'Preparatory School'. This institution had been originally founded by four Oxford graduate sons of a clergyman, pooling their gratuities after the Great War In my day there was just the stern

Mr. Lloyd Senior and the cheerful but sadly crippled Mr. Lloyd Junior. The Messrs Lloyd Minimums and Quartos having departed for other spheres, their places taken by a lady and Mr. Sails, a gifted teacher without any formal qualifications. He was a devotee of Standard cars, even having a 'Flying Standard' a rakish range produced in the mid thirties in an attempt to revive their flagging fortunes. It is sad that this marque with its Union Jack badge was a victim of etymology. When the name was chosen 'Standard' inferred the acme of quality – the Gold Standard, the Standard yard, the Standard pint brand, later of course Standard ca\me to mean the bottom of the pile a quality far below such as Super or De Luxe. Even more sadly the much-liked Kirby Sails died at the wheel of a Standard Vanguard, the last manifestation of a proud product.

Mr. Lloyd Senior angered easily but fortunately he carried an 'Early Warning System' which was a piece of shrapnel removed from an undisclosed part of his anatomy following the battle of the Somme. This souvenir was attached to his watch chain and when displeased he would spin it, the rate of rotation being proportionate to the height of his displeasure. Mr John, as Mr Lloyd Junior was informally called despite ongoing pain had a most jolly and optimistic outlook. Miss Lewis the first of the lady teachers was a charmer, curiously always addressed, as were her male colleagues, as 'Sir'. When she left to get married she was replaced by a lady who gave the impression that she hated little boys, and thinking what we were like who could blame her?

I immediately took to this new school, there were no girls. Girls were after all pretty stupid, stuck up and generally useless – and it was so unfair they were allowed to hit you but you must not hit them. On the other hand the boys were not much cop. There were some who were quite intelligent and likeable but many whom were not, particularly those that came from families enjoying newfound wealth.

My secondary education was in a state school, the Grammar School no less, but still a State School, entrance to which was by exam, the 'Scholarship' or 'Skol' or, it was rumoured, by 'pulling strings'.

I had been warned that, going to a 'municipal' school I would be mixing with 'rough and nasty boys'. While indeed a tiny minority were a tad uncouth, in the posh preparatory school I had come from, yobs had almost predominated. In fact the only really nasty piece of work I recall at the Grammar School had previously attended a private school.

The 'Gram' although subsumed into the state system, could somewhat tenuously trace itself back to a 17th century foundation by a cleric named Gore, an otherwise unremarkable Bishop of Waterford (Anglican that is, of course). This gave it a standing that set it apart from the other two jumped up secondary institutions. More importantly the building, or the more immediately visible part of the building, was 19th century mock Tudor, aping the dreaming Oxbridge spires. This manifestly set us apart from the Education Act learning-factory architecture of the Mun Sec (Municipal

Secondary) as Dynevor School was known and certainly from the exiguous timber of the Glanmor Cowsheds. However since at the 'Gram', the ecclesiastical stone and tracery concealed Potemkin Village-like, a range of equally wooden classrooms, the cowshed epithet had to be uttered with caution.

Unlike the other two boys' institutions (an appropriate description), which had (fiercely segregated) girls' departments, we had no female adjacency. Our own counterpart was the High School, a sort of seraglio a mile distant, whose pupils, despite having neither antecedents nor architecture to support the claim, considered themselves superior to the other young ladies' academies. To us any distinction rested on their wearing slit-sided gymslips that occasionally afforded an inflaming glimpse of stocking-top.

Our school, uniquely held Saturday morning classes in exchange for a 'Games Afternoon' on Wednesdays. The 'games' consisted in winter of either playing or watching rugby on Townhill, an eminence that whilst not quite of Alpine elevation was the highest, windiest and coldest part of the town. Watching was infinitely preferable to playing, since after the steep hike to this summit, one was too exhausted to run about and exchanging one's overcoat, cap and scarf, for a shirt and flimsy shorts was deeply unappealing. Besides which the spectator kept himself tolerably clean and his scrotum immune from in-scrum grasping.

Faithful to my 'Muddied oafs and flannelled fools' attitude towards sport, I do not recall having any connection with the summer cricket either, or indeed any recollection of where this infinitely boring activity was carried out. Again, ennui apart, to deliberately face a missile being hurled at one with felonious intent having only a piece of timber for protection seemed foolhardy, although perhaps not as foolhardy as using one's bare hands to arrest in mid-air what was in effect a small cannon ball.

I had a brief affair with the tennis court not just because the balls were softer, but for the opportunity it gave to mix with girls and bare-thighed girls at that. However being repeatedly and humiliatingly defeated by them soon discouraged this activity. I did later take up hockey – mixed hockey – this was immeasurably preferable to rugby, for starters one had a weapon with which to defend oneself, but more importantly there was the possibility of an accidental collision with a charmingly bouncy bosom.

The school had a fine academic record, State Scholarships to Jesus College, Oxford being routine and many old boys achieved eminence and titles; thanks to dedicated teachers, but with little thanks to 'Pinky' the headmaster. He was clearly terrified of his staff from the janitor upwards, and any boy whose father held any municipal position was accorded fawning deference. He almost prostrated himself in front of one boy whose father was an Inspector of Schools. As regards the rest of the pupils, he stormed and screamed at them in a most alarming fashion. Immediate expulsion was his punishment for even the slightest misdemeanour, but since he kept no record and could never put a name to a face, no one actually left. He had a knack of painting himself into a corner, on one occasion something had occurred that had apparently caused him especial displeasure and an emergency assembly of the whole school was called. The headmaster swept onto the platform, pulled his gown around himself with an angry jerk and without naming the offender or specifying the offence, demanded that the culprit stand up. When this produced no result he announced that he knew who the boy was and that unless he owned up he would be in even more serious trouble. With yet again no response he announced that if the boy was not man enough to own up in five seconds he would name and shame him in front of the whole school. He stood in pin-drop silence for the best part of a minute before fleeing red-faced from the hall.

The non-wearing of school caps was a particular no-no to him and he once stated at assembly that he would be waiting at the school gate the next morning and in tones redolent of a hell-fire preacher condemning a serial adulterer, outlined the damnation that would befall any bare-headed boy. His incoherent tantrum when a boy appeared the next day in a trilby hat (which was raised in deferential greeting) was joy to behold.

On another occasion he hauled me out of the class to inform me that my father had been up to some trickery to avoid paying my fees therefore I could consider myself expelled. I obviously just returned to my seat. The facts I discovered were that when remitting the fees my father had put the wrong cheque in the envelope so the Education department of the Council received a cheque for the Electricity department of the Council. As a member of the same Rotary Club as my father, it was a problem that Pinky might have handled better.

I had some difficulty after I left the school. It seems Pinky gave my School Certificate to another boy to give to me, when the document did not appear he suggested that I take it up with the boy, but since he could not remember which boy he gave it to, that suggestion was of little help. When I asked him for a copy he stated I would have to tell the Council that I had lost it and pay for a copy. I never did get a Certificate.

Most of the masters were both able and capable but some were not. I suppose 'mixed ability' would be the kindest term, it being supposed that just as all schools had to take stupid pupils as well as bright ones, so it seemed to be with teachers. The good teachers were liked, the inadequate ones were not. The good ones had affectionate nicknames, the rest tended toward the pejorative. The good ones were called such things as. 'Little Dai', 'Joni Moc', 'Grandpa Gwyn', 'Sperksie', 'Danny', 'Wee Willy' contrasting with the less kindly epithets for the duds.

There were a few whose sapience was below par. On one occasion I recall the boy next to me took advantage of the master's back being turned to raise himself from his seat, 'Let one go', calling out in a loud voice, 'Richards, you dirty bugger'. The master should have realised that there was only one boy in the class, nay in the school, who could have been responsible for such a window-rattler. Nevertheless it was I who was made to stand outside in corridor. I became quite friendly with that master in later life and I conceded on reflection that I ought to have felt flattered at having been confused with the *Cum Lade* anal virtuoso of the school.

There was considerable class distinction amongst the boys. Parental wealth did play some part, a father with a car carried some kudos, as also did one boy, Benson whose father Herbert, apparently had his pencils specially made with his initials on them. But my recollection is that status was derived, not as the books would have it, captaining the first fifteen, or hitting the winning six just seconds before light stopped play, but from more tangible achievements. Prowess at belching and farting were well regarded particularly if either could be done on demand, but one classmate who could urinate into a high-level flush-tank in the boys' toilets enjoyed the highest esteem. But even he had to yield to the lad who claim that his father had a 'fancy woman' conferred unassailable eminence. The kudos was diminished by the discovery that she was not some sleek houri all legs and lipstick, but was in fact a rotund, bespectacled lady of indeterminate age.

I lacked all these attributes, but I was cognisant with one little known fact that earned me some respect from my peers – I knew that girls farted.

I learned this from a girl of about my own age, daughter of a widowed friend of my parents. Although this girl was reserved and proper in other respects, she did unashamedly break wind. In fact well into her teens her knicker-rippers were legendary. I still wonder if this accounts for such an attractive, intelligent and vivacious woman remaining unmarried well into middle age, by which time presumably the mellifluence had mellowed.

8

Families and Feuds

What nonsense is Romeo & Juliet, if Shakespeare had lived in the real world he would have known that Montagues and Capulets would not have fought each other but would have fought amongst themselves. Mercutio would have been more likely to have been run through by a cousin than a Capulet. Anyway my father's family lived locally while my mother's were 300 miles away so swordplay between them would have been impracticable, but backstabbing within each family was routine.

My father's forebears were solid 'Sir Gar' (Carmarthenshire) based from way back. Obviously farming loomed large in their 'CVs' since everyone proudly described themselves as 'Farmers' even if their holding was limited to a pig on a postage stamp. On his mother's side many embraced either blacksmithing or preaching, the latter mainly of the Presbyterian Hellfire variety. The two professions represented opposites sides of the same coin. Ministers were in touch with the Almighty, while blacksmiths because of their fiery associations were assumed to have connections with the Devil. However it must be said that a community might get by without a minister they could not survive without a blacksmith, so the latter lived somewhat more affluently.

My father's mother Esther was one of the five

formidable daughters of Thomas and Mary Jones of the Priory Foundry at Carmarthen. Thomas was born in 1818 (The eldest of 10 children) and died in 1892, thus his life spanned a remarkable era. When he was born the country was reeling from the cost of the French Wars, by the time of his death, Britain had become, largely due to the steam engine, the most prosperous nation on earth.

Thomas' father Benjamin was born in 1794 a blacksmith of Llanpumsaint, by trade but most his income came from the shoeing of cattle being driven to London. Cattle were shod lying down, thus in addition to a blacksmith's brawn cattle farriers required strength of will as well as of arm to persuade a steer which had no wish to lie down that it might be a good idea to do so.

Thomas learned the trade under his father, but in his thirties he recognised that the coming of the railways would end cattle droving and at the same time benefit agriculture, creating a demand for farm machinery and other iron goods. Accordingly he struck out on his own, moving to Carmarthen and taking over the Priory Foundry. Legend has it that when Benjamin died his wife Rachel took over the anvil, but it is more likely that Thomas' brothers did the work under her management. Either way Rachel must have been a formidable woman, curiously her even more formidable daughter-in-law Mary took on the Foundry when her husband Thomas died. Mary was a hard nut, when her grandsons Charlie and Tom Morgan were live-in apprentices, they complained of a near-starvation regime that would have made a Dickensian workhouse see sybaritic.

My father's recorded maternal family history goes back to the 17th century to David Thomas, 'Poet of Llanpumsaint' his 4 x great grandfather born in 1698. David married a Lydia Job. They had a number of children amongst them a son in 1736 whom they called Job after his mother and as was the custom at the time taking his father's Christian name David as a surname. Job married Esther (Jones?) and their daughter Rachel born in 1796 married the above mentioned Benjamin Jones.

It is interesting that at a time when 'Threescore years and ten' was regarded as an age limit, David Thomas lived to be 87, Job David 98, Daniel Job 84, but the longevity genes did not persist The offspring of Rachel's sister Mary who married William Owen a cattle-shoeing blacksmith of Rhydargauau, all died young, included two Presbyterian ministers. One of her brothers, David emigrated to the USA as a Mormon under the surname of Davis and founded the big Chicago dairy machinery firm that bore his adopted name. More notably another brother Thomas followed him retaining the surname of Job and was with Brigham Young on the Great Trek and was a co-founder of Salt Lake City.

Leaving Tom and Mary Jones for the moment and looking at my father's paternal side. They were mostly farmers, his great great grandfather being Tomas Davies who had a son William Davies. But when it came to his son also William born 1812 (My father's grandfather) he went under the surname of Richards, the cognominal *non sequitter* being due to William senior adopting the name Richards, allegedly in acknowledgement of a legacy.

William Junior married a Margaret Harris and took on a small farm Llwynmartin Isa, a melodic name in Welsh but translates into English regrettably as 'Martin's lower bush'. This must have been something of a comedown for Margaret since her folk farmed in a substantial way and being Abergwili based had better land than Llwynmartin Isa in Llanpumsaint.

Unfortunately he died in 1854 aged only 42, leaving Margaret with three children John 7, Elizabeth 2 and Anne an infant. Margaret struggled to keep going with the help of a maidservant. After a year or so she found she was unable to cope with even the few pathetic acres so had to take on a man David Jones to do the heavy work. Either through affection or economic necessity, she married him and in 1859 they had a little girl, Mary. Tragically on a bleak November Tuesday the baby scarcely 5 weeks old, succumbed to a fever. The following Saturday that same fever claimed her daughter Elizabeth now aged 7. The following year Margaret herself died giving birth to a son, attended, if at all, by a 'Wise Woman', who would be some old crone of a pseudo midwife. Presumably there were complications, and she undoubtedly died slowly and in agony.

Jones immediately married the maid, giving rise to speculation that this was merely regularising an arrangement that had occurred during Margaret's pregnancy, but it is just as likely that he had realised that if he married the girl he could stop paying her! The trouble was that the new Mrs Jones jibbed at caring for children that were not even her husband's and ordered the two surviving Richards children, John aged 13 and Ann aged 6, out of the house. Family legend has it that they trekked some dozen footsore miles, Anne clutched the rag doll, her sole memento of her mother, while John carried the rest of their meagre possessions in a makeshift parcel. They ended up staving, wet and exhausted on the doorstep of their uncle John Harris, their mother's brother.

When uncle John died shortly afterwards his widow Mary kept Ann but passed young John to William Harris, her late husband's brother who in due course sent the boy to the boomtown of Merthyr Tydfil, where his son Evan was apprenticed to a Pharmacist, to learn the grocery trade. When John Richards married Esther Jones, it was from William Harris' home. It was a 'Bidding' wedding, allegedly the last in Carmarthenshire. In the case of a Bidding wedding a Bidder goes around the village bidding neighbours to bring bedding, furniture, cooking pots – everything the happy couple would need to set up a home. This seems a big improvement on the modern multi toast-rack and fondue set custom of more modern times. What is more it was implicit that all items or their worth had to be returned to the giver within a year and a day.

To revert to my father's maternal side Benjamin and Rachel had 10 children of which the eldest Thomas and the youngest Catherine impinge upon our radar.

Thomas and Mary Jones of the Foundry had eleven children and it was edicted by Mary that all her children's first-born sons were to be called Thomas after her husband and the first-born daughters Mary after herself. Fortunately for family historians the potential 11 cousins called Thomas and another 11 called Mary did not, due to death or disobedience, materialise but there were still an awful lot of both.

I have little or no knowledge of the two sons of Thomas and Mary, John and Benjamin who survived into the 20th century. I do recall the wedding of Benjamin's daughter Mary in 1933 since it was the first wedding I attended. It was in Bethesda Welsh Baptist chapel at Swansea, where John Richards, my grandfather had been a deacon. The bride was 'given away' by my father, a concept I had some difficulty in grasping. Records show that she was 47 and married Thomas Randall 55, a Marine Engineer of Pontarddulais who was the son of Richard Randall a tinplate works superintendent.

The daughters of Thomas and Mary Jones (The formidable Foundry Five) formed the core of my father's family. The eldest who became a Mrs Evans was only a name to me and Harriet (Mrs Williams), I only knew as a tiny child when as a widow she lived with her twin sister Ann, whom elderly relatives called the 'Terrible Twins'. Their sister Mary who became Mrs James Rees only minimally impinged on me, Ann, the twice married Mrs Morgan/Price) most certainly did. Oddly the closest of them Esther, my grandmother Mrs John Richards, I never knew since she died before I was born.

These latter three ladies produced a trio of Thomas'. To avoid confusion my father Thomas William Richards was called 'Teedoubleyou'. Thomas John Rees was called 'Teejay', but Thomas Morgan the son of Ann Morgan/Price having three initials Teejayess' was considered too much of a mouthful so he uniquely was allowed to remain Tom, Tom's mother was the only one of these formidable ladies that I vividly remember, I could never get my head around why she was called 'Aunty Price' when her son's name was Morgan.

When in 1874 Esther married John Richards now an experienced grocer, Thomas and Mary Jones set them up as a Butter Merchants in Swansea. This was a shrewd move creating an outlet in an expanding town for produce from relatives' farms north of Carmarthen, the opening of the 'Manchester & Milford' Railway in 1867 having made this feasible, serving as it did the Llanpumsaint area.

John and Esther had five children, my father Thomas William, my Uncle David who died long before I was born, my Aunty Mary Ann and my Uncle John Sydenham (John S.). Another daughter, Louise, died in infancy.

I was well aware that my parents did not 'Get on' with my uncles and aunts and while it would have been an exaggeration to say that everyone hated everyone else, it was a good working hypothesis. However it took decades for me to sort out all the nuances.

For starters my aunt Mary Ann (Marion), my father's sister with whom he lodged never entirely forgave him for bedding and wedding (in that order) the 'Dreadful Widow Williams' (my mother) similarly she bore a life-long grudge against the DWW for having 'stolen their

Tom' (that is to say my father not the cat), these feelings being reciprocated in spades.

Mary Ann's husband was the redoubtable Uncle Pricey, widely famed for his extreme financial prudence (It was said at his funeral that if he had known that 'he could not take it with him', he would not have gone); and for the pungency of his 'roll-up' cigarettes.

These attributes sometimes caused his distinction to be forgotten – he was not only a Master Mariner but having sailed 'before the mast' beyond 40 degrees south in a windjammer, he was also a genuine Cape Horner.

He was descended from a Carmarthenshire family of master weavers whose fortunes allegedly originated from prize money won fighting with Nelson at Copenhagen. His father was the formidable Reverend County Councillor Henry (Smyrna) Jones. Having as a young man acted as a lay preacher at Smryna Chapel, Llangain, he decided to wear the Cloth rather than make it, so adopting the name Smyrna he trained at Bala College for the Presbyterian pastorship.

Oddly his first call was to Bosra Welsh Independent (Congregational) Capel Pensa' waun, Llandeiniolen. While on circuit from there he met and married (in Swansea) Harriet (Hettie) daughter of Catherine Evans, sister of Tom Jones of the Foundry. Pricey was born in Llandeiniolen but was raised at Llangefni Anglesey where his father combined tending a smallholding with the pastorship of Sardis, Bodfforff and Ebenezer, Rhosmeirch (both near Llangefni). He and his wife Hattie had a further two sons and two daughters as well as adopting an orphaned brother and sister, also providing accommodation in their home for up to eight of the workers in the stocking factory which Hettie ran for 'battered wives', as well as a wool shop in Llangefni that would later be run by Caroline, wife of their youngest son Henry (Ted). Henry took on the farm and the shop, they had three children Henry III, Mair and Alun (named after me).

Shortly before WW1 Uncle Pricey joined a Swansea-based ship, so it was natural that Esther should allow her cousin's son to board and lodge under her roof. It must have been a squeeze since the house at 9 Gore Terrace also housed her sons Tom and John S, her daughter Mary Ann and the maid Annie 'King's Head' So named after the Llangafellach pub where she was brought up.

As I would discover many years later, having a lusty sailor in the same house as a daughter fast approaching her wed-by date, the inevitable happened. Uncle Pricey 'did the right thing' and married Mary Ann, another little soul wags added to the household head count, 'Little Louise'. Unfortunately the happy couple did not leave to set up their own *ménage*, but stayed put.

The presence of a cuckoo in the nest must have spurred John S to fly the nest. He married May John and set up house at Trinity Place a smart address near Gore Terrace, where they proceeded to raise four daughters. Sadly one died but the other three (the youngest a year or two older than me) grew into lively and charming girls, a complete contrast to the chestnut-haired suet pudding that was their cousin Louise. Pricey and Mary Ann never forgave John S and May for having the effrontery to produce daughters that were prettier and manifestly cleverer than theirs. Again there was an automatic reciprocation of sentiment.

I imagine that the departure of John S must have been hastened by the 'Two-tomcats-in-a-bag' situation of the two brothers living in the same house. The tension had its roots way back in 1908. John S had been a 'late extra' so that the family was described as the Boys (Tom & David), Mary Ann and John S, relegating John S to hermaphrodite status. When old John Richards died in 1902, John S struck out on his own to make a professional career, leaving Tom and David to 'mind the shop'.

Group pictures of David in Glamorgan Volunteers Uniform show him wearing his pillbox at a jauntier angle than his brother Tom. His diaries reveal that he was in the habit of walking young ladies to the less populous but more arboreal parts of the town, Singleton Park then a private estate, being a favoured destination.

Diaries also hint that these trips rarely lacked a 'Happy Ending'. He was the enthusiastic owner of a De Dion-Bouton motorcar and Frank Reed who remained with the firm as foreman driver/mechanic until the 1950s was the 'reserve power' for hill climbing. He recalled how on gradients gentlemen would cover ladies ears as David exhorted him to 'Push harder for f---s sake'.

Despite the somewhat laid-back even rakish image, when on a recuperative cruise to Egypt following persistent ill health, it became apparent that it was he not Tom who was the mover and shaker. Tom having been apprenticed to a Ferndale, Rhondda grocer undoubtedly could cut bacon or weigh out sugar, but he was no businessman. Consequently when in 1908 David died, having outlived his father by scarcely a twelvemonth, mother Esther ordered John S to come home and take David's place. John S who having qualified was carving out a career as an agricultural auctioneer at Tywyn Merionethshire, was to say the least not best pleased.

When the old lady died in 1922 her estate was divided equally between the three. Tom, John S and Mary Ann. What happened about John's moiety I do not know, but when Tom married in 1923 he had at least as much right as his sister to the 9 Gore Terrace House but Mary Ann and Pricey sat tight forcing Tom to buy himself a house on the crest of the post-war boom which within a year or two all but halved in value. I doubt if the Price Jones ever bought out Tom's share but if they did it would undoubtedly have been based on the few hundred that their late father had paid for it 20 years before.

9

Relations with Relations

Whether John S forgave his mother for forcing him to give a up a job he liked in a desirable part of the world, I do not know, but he certainly never forgave his brother Tom whose perceived shortcomings caused her to do so.

John S proved an innovative and energetic entrepreneur installing packing machinery and developing and promoting 'Investa' flour and other packed groceries.

Following unsuccessful attempts to make deliveries with a bus scrapped by the General Omnibus Company of London, in 1912 he bought a Milnes-Daimler 1½-tonr lorry (Built by the Daimler Company of Berlin and marketed in the UK by Messrs Milnes). This was followed by an Albion and a 4-ton Leyland and in 1919 by a similar Leyland ex-RAF.

Having transport, the firm participated in the 1917 Motor Volunteer Corps whereby firms and individuals supplied vehicles and drivers, the latter being given a denim uniform, to hold themselves in readiness should movement of men and materiel be required. There were also facilities for men to be taught to drive under this scheme. I believe that my father availed himself of this, but with what success is unknown.

It must have riled my father to play second fiddle to a brother younger and shorter than himself. On the other hand John S was not over the moon when having prospered during WW1 Tom 'invested' a wedge of the firm's cash in a non-existent oil company. On top of that, a traveller trousered a serious slice of the firm's takings which John S attributed to his brother's lack of vigilance.

My father clearly was more a boulevardier than a businessman and when Pricey returned from the Navy and obtained a post as a Swansea Sea Pilot the prospect of permanently putting up with Pricey (and Mary Ann!) at home and his brother at work must have seemed unappealing. On top of which his mother, Esther died, leaving him without an ally.

He solved the problem by turning up one day having covertly married in a London Registry Office, and as has been said, set up house. John S almost immediately demanded to be bought out and set up his own business wholesaling matting and hardware. He did not choose the most appropriate time since the post-war boom had collapsed, seriously affecting the firm's profitability and my father with a new wife and baby in an overpriced house.

Unaware of all this I could only view Uncle John S and his family from afar, since they never visited our house nor, until I was a teenage, did we visit theirs. I knew Uncle John S to be as short of fuse as he was of stature, but despite the infrequency of contact John S was a source of aphorisms that have stood me in good stead throughout my life. His urging me never to be afraid to speak to a public figure since he dare not admit not knowing you, has gained me entrance to the Irish Dail as the guest of De Valera and acquaintance with many of the great and the good. His advice never to hesitate to enter an open door has given me entry to many interesting places and indeed resulted in many friendships.

Moreover he had a CAR! Not the ordinary 7 or 8 horsepower Austin or Morris but a 28 horse power American Dodge. He conned this charabanc-sized vehicle by peering through the steering wheel, with his much taller wife acting as a sort of periscope lookout, whilst the three daughters giggled side by side on the sofa-sized back seat.

These three sisters could not have been more different, Nora the eldest, half a dozen year older than me, was the academic who married Cliff Bowen the clergyman son of the managing director of the Swansea and Mumbles Railway. She would be tragically widowed with four young sons.

The youngest girl, Beryl, a couple of years older than me was the exuberant one, her husband Peter Lowrie became very senior in electrical engineering and they would have two sons and a daughter. The 'middle' daughter Muriel would go on to marry mechanically gifted Jim Hitchings and have two sons. One of whom was to achieve international standing as an electronics academic. Just as John S had been ordered home to run John Richards Ltd, so Muriel and her husband would be ordered home by John S to help run his business cutting short Jim's promising career on busies machines.

We for some reason saw more of the 'Gore Terrace People', Pricey, Mary Ann and Louise.

Pricey although not ungenerous towards me, (He once bought me a Fairy Cycle but having won a share in a big sweepstake was drunk at the time) he lived up to his reputation for extreme financial prudence, his one extravagance being chain-smoking roll-ups of quite singular pungency. It was many years before I connected his tobacco supply with my trips on the pilot boat, Roger Beck. On these I would go aboard with him at the docks but at the end of the day would be landed by rowing boat at Mumbles, always being entrusted with a little parcel, which he would collect from our house in the evening. I was a willing party to this since he would give me a shilling (5p) for the Mumbles Train. Since the fare was no more than 6d (2½p) this gave me a profit representing three-quarters of a pound of Woolworth's Pick & Mix, or six Milky Ways or three Mars Bars, these latter at 2d each being normally beyond the reach of all but the most affluent of children. I would incidentally spend much of my 'sea time' on the bridge standing on a beer crate steering the boat to enable the Skipper to go below to join the pilots' card school.

Uncle Pricey had acquired a number of skills as a deep-sea apprentice, but since it had been in sailing vessels his knowledge of such things as amps and volts was limited. Despite this, he was constantly making modifications and augmentations to the electrical arrangements at home, as a result it was wise to use one's sleeve as an insulator when touching a switch, bell push or any other item of an electrical nature. He had found that nails were more reliable than fuse wire, so that any electrical malfunction was liable to be spectacular, it being not unknown for his tinkering to deprive the whole street of supply.

He did eventually have a car – none of brother-in-law John S's ostentatious Yankee rubbish for him, he bought a stately Wolseley 12-48, reassuringly larger and newer than the Austin 10, which his other brother-in-law, my father, drove. Pricey's approach to maintenance was robust. As a seaman he realised that rust must be chiselled away and replaced with red-lead paint. Thus within a few years his vehicle resembled a psychedelic leopard. He believed that oil changes were a marketing ploy by the lubricant manufactures so that the vehicle sounded like a bag of agitated spanners and was followed by a plume of white smoke redolent of a Papal election.

His wife, my Aunty Mary Ann, I would hesitate to call mean since she did sometimes give me a ½d bar of Cadbury's Dairy Milk Chocolate, the peculiar taste of which I deduced later, was caused by long-term storage in a clothes drawer. Since milk chocolate was considered unhealthy, I was not to know until much later that milk chocolate did not necessarily taste of mothballs. This apart, she pushed the frontiers of thriftiness into virgin territory. She did send cards at Christmas but her signature was invariably on a distressed area where the name of the original sender had been bleached and scratched.

She had inherited her maid from her mother Esther. Annie served Esther and then Mary Ann for 50 years allegedly without a pay rise. Despite her indigency when I left to join the RAF she pressed a 10/- (50p) note, possibly a week's pay. She died still in service, leaving her pathetically small life savings to a niece. Yet I recall

Pricey and Mary Ann saying that since' they had been so good to her over the years, she should have left something to them! Mary Ann did not buy clothes either for herself or her daughter Louise, but had them 'Run up' by a little woman who shared an upstairs alcove with what was said to be one of Mr. Singer's first sewing machines.

Louise, the cause of the hasty matrimony was some thirteen years older and took a near-motherly interest in me constantly warning me of the dangers of this world. These dangers were not for instance being run over by a tram, but were of a more subtle nature. Apparently there were girls who 'Went the whole hog', I did eventually discover what she meant, but the dangers they posed remained obscure – I did try to get her to tell me where such girls might be found, but despite making it crystal clear that I needed to know so that such locations could be avoided, she never would tell me. She shared her mother's economic theories and in later life attended lectures and similar functions with a carrier bag into which a plate of snacks could be deftly tipped.

To move on beyond my father's siblings, further into this warp and weft of intermarriage and intrigue, we must remain with those stout (in both senses) daughters of the foundry, the next of whom was Esther's sister Mary. She married a James Rees and her parents set them up as bakers and grocers in Baptist Well Street, Swansea. This was done a couple of years before John and Esther Richards were set up in Union Street. It may be that the success of the Rees retail shop emboldened Thomas and

Mary Jones to make the Richards' wholesalers.

Surprisingly we had almost nothing to do with them and I scarcely ever me their eldest son Teejay Rees Director of Education and disciple of grain and grape, was a few years older than my father. He had daughters and grand daughters who did well in life, one daughter marrying Dr. Morton the much respected Reynoldston G.P.

Teejay's brother Fred died before my time but we saw a great deal of his widow and daughter, an inseparable couple nicknamed 'Gert & Daisy'. Mother Alice and daughter Yosé floated around like undecided votes, one never seen without the other. Being the same age Yosé and I were seen as potential material by the matchmakers of the family, but it was only after her mother died that she saw herself as eligible. She had the good sense to marry a rather wealthy older man whose early demise left her free to remarry a younger man and become the terror of the *Thés Dansat* of Torquay.

The third daughter of the foundry was the twice-widowed Ann, confusingly called Aunty Price, she together with her twin sister Harriet oscillated between Ann's son and daughter's residences. The daughter Nancy who as a serial kisser, was seriously unpopular with small boys. She lived in a converted mill on the water's edge of Milford Haven with husband Arthur Rees a very posh grocer who bred Sealyham dogs. They had a son Noel a very jolly bank manager some dozen years older than myself, thus was given the courtesy appellation of 'Uncle'. He married his charming long term 'fiancée' Brenda late in life. Brenda was the training supervisor of telephone operators over a wide area of south Wales, a big responsibility with a manual exchange in almost every town and village of consequence, having scores of operators. Arthur and Nancy besides catering to the *crachach* (snobs) of the county and breeding Crufts champions were the backbone of the 'Smart Set', a Glee Party who gave concerts in the large country houses. As a child I saw a lot of Noel since he worked in Swansea and lodged at Gore Terrace with the Price Jones'. When he returned to Neyland he took over the family residence and although the 'Smart Set' had long gone he and Brenda sang publicly for charity events.

If there was one thing that could unite my father's family in common cause, it was dislike of Nancy's brother Tom Morgan. Tom and his brother Charlie, following apprenticeships at the Foundry, set up in Swansea as Morgan Bros 'Electrical Engineers'. Charlie left and opened his own business in Liverpool, leaving Tom to carry on.

As a youngster I thought Uncle Tom was great, he was certainly 'good with children' and indeed he had a child-like enthusiasm for everything at work or play. He lived above his electrical shop in Mansel Street with his wife Bessie, a son, two daughters, and from time to time his mother and Harriet (Bessie thus had two mothers-in-law!) He was the first of his generation to have a car, not an ordinary car but a badge of success a Rover rightly then known as the businessman's Rolls Royce.

He had many failings but excessive modesty was not one of them. I recall him visiting America and many years later being shown a cutting from a Chicago newspaper, which reported the visit of this 'Great electrical engineer who had just spent a million British pounds lighting the whole of the great city of Swansea'.

Tom Morgan was a Rotarian, but unlike my father, uncle John S and Uncle Teejay to whom Rotary was a vaguely good cause luncheon club, he espoused it with a quite astonishing fervour. Indeed he espoused everything with fervour, taking up such movements as 'Moral rearmament' that abounded in the 1930s. He also 'took up' things in business – he was a pioneer protagonist of washing machines – the great clanking wood and cast iron 'Beatty', reminiscent of its namesake Admiral's battleships ('You can't Beat a Beatty'). When the Bendix automatic washing machine was introduced by a retail competitor he proclaimed from these machines – 'Automatically washed, automatically dried, and automatically goes out of order'. A slogan hastily withdrawn when he obtained the Bendix agency for himself.

I do not recall either he or his wife Bessie, and certainly nor his son Ronnie or his two daughters ever being in our house nor we visiting theirs. For that matter, I do not recall May and John S visiting us but later after the detestation juices had mellowed we did visit them. On the other hand visits from Mary Ann and Pricey and vice-versa were routine.

Pricey, stood aloof from our family feuds, probably because he had family feuds of his own, reserving his detestations for his own siblings. He did receive visits from his younger brother Ted and his family (I recall being shocked when before being hurried away, I glimpsed his wife holding baby Mair and actually putting one of her bosoms in its mouth!). The rest of them he never mentioned except his sister Bea (Lyle), who was the only one in Swansea. He was constantly reviling her, her husband and her two daughters at every opportunity.

Pricey did on one occasion show his aloofness from his wife's relationship issues by buying a Beatty washing machine from Tom Morgan. It was the latest model with a powered wringer whose rollers were warranted to accept fabric but reject a finger. I was present when Pricey demonstrated the effectiveness of this safety feature – far from rejecting his finger it accepted it – up to his armpit! Pricey hastily joined the Tom Morgan basher ranks.

I recall the day when any chance of a John S/May and Tom/Bessie *rapprochement* was totally wrecked. Tom Morgan lived above the hop in Mansel Street; John S lived in Trinity Place, a street that had 'Gone down' as residential address. John S moved upmarket to a fine detached house bordering on smart Sketty. Then one morning John S went out of his front door to see Bessie not only emerging from the front door opposite, but also shaking a mat! The rift became irreparable.

So what was the case of this Great Schism? I was baffled for years. Apparently in 1908, 30 and more years earlier Esther arranged for electric lighting to be installed in Bethesda chapel as a memorial to her late husband John. So what was more natural than to entrust the work to her nephew Tom Morgan. Allegedly, he messed up the job and overcharged! The feud lasted the lifetime of the parties involved.

For me any Tom Morgan admiration was ended when during the war at a Rotary Club, 'Sons and daughters day', Tom gave a speech of welcome to the said sons and daughters. After some hyperbolic wanderings, he talked about his own son Ronnie whom he described as a 'Hero deserving a medal' for his electrical work on ships in the docks (and getting very well paid for it!) He waxed lyrically how, despite bombs raining down on him, he carried on his great work, (There had not been a bomb dropped on Swansea docks for 3 years!). Despite a palpable undercurrent of anger from members who had sons fighting in Italy, the Far East and over Germany, he crassly carried on. When I saw the distress he was causing to men who had a son in prison camps in Germany and Japan, I vowed to have nothing to do with Tom Morgan (or with Rotary).

In Wales in particular there is the difficulty in comprehending relationships since the titles, uncle and aunt are conferred not just on parents siblings and their spouses, but also on even the most distantly related person and indeed on adults who are no relation at all.

One such honorary uncle (actually the great grandson of Margaret, a sister of Thomas Jones, the Foundry) was Iorwerth Davies, who despite living in Neath seemed to be on the periphery of every family gathering (Those rare occasions when enough members of the family were on speaking terms to form a bona fide gathering). 'Uncle Iorwerth' was a bank manger and dressed like a Bank Manager. On even the most informal occasion, he would no more be seen without his bowler hat and umbrella than he would go out without his black jacket and striped trousers.

Also prominent on the periphery was that notable cleric the redoubtable Reverend 'Uncle' Ben Jones Vicar of Llanrhidian, ('Hide the cheese, Ben's coming up the path!'). He lived terrorised by his wife Maggie and daughter Gwenfil in reputedly the dampest and draughtiest vicarage in the Diocese. He was a 'double descendant of the Foundry his father David being the son of, brother of Thomas Jones and his first wife Rachel, and of Mary daughter of Thomas Jones' sister Harriet.

The thrice-married John Jones worked as a blacksmith with his brother Thomas at the Foundry. He for a time ran the New King George Inn, Priory Street Carmarthen (Presumably it opened shortly followed the 1820 accession of George IV). Being adjacent to the foundry, it is alleged that the proximity caused the eventual downfall of the foundry, its profits having been discharged against its the back wall. It is believed that this example was the source of the rabid teetotalism of John Jones' great nephew John S. Richards.

The 'Rev Ben' mother was Mary Lewis who was the daughter of Benjamin Lewis who married Hannah another sister of Tom Jones. The Rev. Ben was a noted Hebrew scholar, but used to boast that his greatest achievement was winning the John Bull 'Bullets' contest.

(This weekly paper ran a competition for the pithiest says about a given phase. His, 'Actresses Jewels' was as far as I recall. 'If chaste, paste'.) He was also a Bachelor of Divinity an unusual qualification for a church clergyman. Unusually for a woman the same degree was held by Nora Bowen eldest daughter of John S Richards. Equally unusual was her knowledge of both classical and modern Greek.

Gwenfil, 'Rev Ben's' daughter who was born c 1920 attended the High School with Muriel Hitchings (Née Richards) married Geoffrey Matthew Chief Medical Officer to Richard Thomas Ltd the steel and tinplate firm

Ever present at the extremity of my perception were the Harris', the family of Margaret whose orphaned children, John and Ann Richards, they fostered. I had always wondered why it was that Henry Harris the tenant of Singleton Home Farm, (now a Council depot) and grazed sheep in Singleton Park up to his death in 1942, had an interest in John Richards Ltd. I was delighted to find that Henry was the son of John Harris who had first taken in the two children and that when his firm was incorporated in 1902; John Richards had given Henry a block of shares in gratitude.

Henry would never kill a fox, but trapped them and kept them in captivity. I have always hoped that the rumour that he sold them to the Penllegaer Hunt to provide a quarry for their hounds to chase and tear apart, was untrue.

It was the descendants of another Henry, brother to

John and William with whom I came into contact. Jane, one of the daughters of Henry and his wife Elizabeth married the Rev. D. O. Rees, the distinguished minister of Bethel Welsh Congregational chapel, Sketty. We saw a lot of their daughter Olive, headmistress of Sketty School and her brother Bernard whose son David, my contemporary, became a journalist and author and was commissioned by the American Government to write *A Limited War*, the official account of the Korean campaign. Another daughter, Elizabeth trumped her sister by marrying (sequentially!) two ministers, the Rev. Emrys Lloyd and after his death the widowed Rev. Howell Elvet Lewis. The latter was a noted poet and hymn-writer who became Archdruid of Wales 1924-28, he was also a 'Double Doctor' D D & Ll D).

Two of Jane's sisters confused genealogists by married without changing their names – Hetty married a J. O. Harris while Ann married a William Harris, possibly brothers and almost certainly related.

Ann's William farmed Drwyslyn Fawr, where he had a reputation amongst the Gwendraeth colliers as a generous payer for help at busy times. Later he moved to the nearby Glandulais, a magnificent Georgian house with, to me, exciting outbuildings. It had been a big holding but William, due to advancing age retained only a modest 30 acres or so. It was their family that we saw much of.

They had three daughters Margaret, Minnie and Lilly (A son Ernest died young). Minnie married Raymond Oliver a London solicitor with firm Welsh roots and distinguished legal antecedents. They had three sons

Penry and twins John and David. After William died the unmarried sisters let off the land and divided the house. The Oliver family visited every summer arriving in some style sitting in the same seats in their reserved compartment all the way from Euston to Drwyslyn Station. After we had the car we visited them.

The Old Lady (Ann) died before my time but William I remember well. High jinks were liable to ensue, in which a Bath Chair made an ideal Wells Fargo coach to be defended from Indians). It was possible, although perhaps unwise to ride it down the stairs. On one occasion I stayed with the Olivers at Kenton Road Harrow and recall being generously entertained at shows and exhibitions.

After the spinster sisters died John (By then a Judge) took over the house in its entirety for his retirement which having proved sadly brief, the property passed to his widow Frances and her daughter Isobel and her three sons. David (Who with his wife Jose had two sons and three daughters) did not long outlive his twin. Penry a Bristol schoolmaster married to Siận had three sons. He moved to Pembroke to enjoy a sadly short retirement.

My parents' car enabled them to also visit the various Carmarthenshire relations and (with a proper show of reluctance) accept tea and cake. I recall Pentresite, home of Tom Evans nephew of Hettie, (Uncle Pricey's mother); also of Pentrebach a Welsh Longhouse home to the descendants of the second marriage of Mary Harris (John Harris's widow) although relationship was remote; my father never forgot the family of his father's foster mother so our visits were frequent. I remember the old father (Mary's son) sleeping in a cupboard bed. Such beds originated in the time of the one-room dwelling. They enabled elderly relatives to retire earlier than the rest of the family and spared them the embarrassment of witnessing any conjugal activity. Later in the days of sleeping in a crug loft, it spared the elderly person the perils of the ladder, enabled them to remain close to the fire and if animals were brought inside at night, the doors protected them from the importunities of overfriendly cattle or sheep. More importantly it kept them within easy reach of the Tŷ Bach (outside loo).

It was only later that we met up with the 'Llandovery people'. They were the descendants of the Reverend Thomas Thomas who was the son of Esther, sister of Mary, the wife of 'Tom Jones Foundry'. He was a great Calvinist divine, who preached in America during the 1904 'Religious Revival' but still had time to father 13 children. In later life his granddaughter Beryl, her 'larger than life' husband Gwyn and Beryl's niece, Roberta Thomas, became good friends.

One of Rev. 'Tom Tom's' sons took part in the Witwatersrand Gold Rush of 1886 but had the good sense to buy land where there was no gold. Thus he found himself ground landlord of much of Johannesburg!

In the course of these visits some delicacy was required, it being very unwise to mention any other relatives since it was difficult to remember who was not speaking to who and alliances constantly and confusingly waxed and waned like phases of the moon.

Happily these silly postures seem to be dying out and subsequent generations despite (or because of) geographical separation seem all to get on with each other.

10

The Divided Distaff

My mother's family posed fewer contentions, partly possibly because living in Norfolk, distance lent enchantment to my view of them. Nevertheless in a part of most rural England, locked in a 19th if not 18th century time warp, similar feuds and factions existed

We seem to start with John Barrow who was born in Huntingdon in 1795. He married a Mary Porter and living in Southery produced a dozen children between 1817 and 1842, a time spread that made the eldest more like uncles and aunts to the tail-ender siblings. John's third child and eldest son John Henry was born in 1823 marrying a Hilgay girl Eliza Edwards in 1845 and they emigrated to America in 1851. In this quiet backwater the USA was still regarded as a bunch of rebellious colonies, so voluntarily going there must have seemed like undergoing Transportation, without the pleasure of murdering someone or stealing a sheep.

He finished up in Ohio where widowed young, he married a Harriet Babcock. Unlike Old McDonald he did not have a farm but probably was a house painter as was his son Ebenezer Arthur. E.A. received glowing obituaries when he died in 1888 but within this family he is spoken of as 'Mean son of a bitch!' Happily I am in touch with his Great x 3 granddaughters, Billie Carnes

My mother's father Edward Ebenezer was the

youngest of the twelve, He married his mother's namesake and presumed relative, Mary Porter. One of his sisters having in the meantime married a Mr. Porter, (Sounds like the Marie Lloyd song!) all of which seems rather incestuous but all this took place in the Southery area where Barrows and Porters (Sounds like a railway station!) were common names. He set up in West Dereham as Postmaster, draper and grocer. There was at the time a George Barrow, possibly an uncle in a similar business at nearby Hilgay. Mary Barrow II produced two children Arthur and Edward Thomas Ebenezer, but she died young.

Edward Ebenezer married secondly Rachel of West Dereham, daughter of Fredrick and Sarah Steward, who as occupiers of Basil Farm carried some standing in the parish.

The Stewards come into the picture with Fredrick Steward a shoemaker born in Stoke Ferry who in 1841 aged 15 was lodging in West Dereham with James Horn, a carpenter. No record of Fred's background has been traced, but he seems to have had a sister Mary who may have been his twin who was a live-in servant with a family in Stoke Ferry so they may well have been orphaned. The Stewards are said to come from Huntington and to be descended from Elizabeth Steward, mother of Oliver Cromwell. We know nothing of the Horns, except that the name may be an Anglicisation of Hoorn and if so, descend from Dutch engineers who were brought over in the 17th century to cut the Bedford Level and other Fen drainage schemes.

Young Fred seems to have done what lodgers in

limericks do, since in 1851 he was married to Sara, one of the Horn daughters with a son aged 8 and four other children aged 5 down to 1. The age gap between the first-born and the second suggest that following a 'Little accident' the pair of them were kept apart for a couple of years until Fred was considered able to support a wife. The 1841 census show them both as having been born in 1826 the 1851 census shows their birth years as 1823. Presumably it was feared that the census-taker's eyebrow might be raised if the parents of an 8-year old were shown to be 24 or 25. (Since both were born before the Registration of Births Act of 1836, there would be no official record of their ages). Actually there was no question of illegality since the Age of Consent and of marriage, was 12 at the time and even then underage sex only attracted a nominal fine and only if 'Loss of Maidenhood' was involved. However marriage before the man could provide for a wife and family was considered reprehensible.

By this time Fred was describing himself as a farmer. Unless he had had help from the Horns' it is difficult to know how he could have afford the ingoings to take on a farming tenancy, so he may have still been following his trade and assuming the status of 'Farmer' on the strength of a pig or two in the back yard. Anyway that census makes interesting reading, Fred's now widowed mother-in-law describes her occupation not as 'Widow' but as 'Proprietor of House', as if to distinguish herself from mere tenants (such as he son-in-law?). It also records, the 4-year old daughter of Fred and Sara as living with her, (Commonplace in large families until the eldest daughter was old enough to take a share of household chores). Although it was usual in the case of an infant to leave the 'Occupation' box blank, this child is shown as 'Grand daughter of a shoemaker'. Apart from indicating that Fredrick had followed his father's trade, it seems the Mrs Horn felt that her son-in-law was getting above himself in calling himself a farmer.

Fred and Sara went on to have other children including a daughter Rachel and it is interesting that in later life they reverted to their presumably true birth years of 1826. By the early 1880s they were substantial farmers; occupying Basil Farm and Fred was listed as one of the prominent citizens of West Dereham. Landowners do of course prefer their children to make 'Strategic Alliances' with the children of other landowners, the Stewards with a not particularly facially favoured daughter who at 33 was already in 'Old Maid' territory had to accept what was on offer at the time, which happened to be E. E. Barrow.

E. E. B at 40 was 'Getting on a bit', had a teenage son (Only they did not call them that in those days) and was not only a shopkeeper but he was also the Postmaster, a representative of Her Britannic Majesty no less. Whist he was actually only a sub-postmaster he had some extraordinary powers. Once a letter was popped into the post-box it became Royal Mail and until safely delivered was in effect the property of the Queen, hence he had the right to defend the Royal Mail by whatever means and commandeer horses and impress persons to speed it and deal with any miscreant that impeded its passage. Thus their son-in-law although landless, did enjoy some standing, plus there would be the chance of a discount on their groceries!

The other Steward girls were possibly no more glamorous than their sister Rachel as by late 1880s the three youngest were proving to be 'difficult to shift' Rhoda and Sara in their mid 20s were still 'marketable', but Eliza had reached 30 with no takers and was following her parents' example of 'massaging' her date of birth, knocking off 3 years to avoid the dreaded three-oh. Anyway in 1891 she married a William Gentle. Rachel marrying a grocer was bad enough but this alliance smacks of desperation. William, the son of a Hertfordshire publican whom she had presumably met when he was a chain boy with the Ordnance Survey when the 1st Edition of the 6' OS map of west Norfolk was being prepared in 1881. Following a spell in the Cape Colony as a Trooper with the Cape Mounted Rifles, he was now a London Policeman, then regarded as a refuge for men with an adverse Brains to Brawn ratio. What is more he was younger than even her 'revised' age which in those days was not considered ideal. Her parents put a brave face on things but held the marriage discreetly in Downham Market.

The Stewards need not have worried, William Gentle was barely 30 when he was promoted to Superintendent in the Reading Force and well before he was 40 was Chief Constable of Brighton, shortly becoming a national figure due to his having broken up the notorious Brighton racecourse criminal gangs. Knighted in 1916, on retirement he became a successful businessman, chairman of the Greyhound Racing Association and had an interest in Belle Vue Gardens, Manchester. He became a Justice of the Peace and was four times Mayor of Thetford and served as High Sheriff of Norfolk. He is buried in Norwich Cathedral. Their eldest son Frederick born at Basil Farm became Chief Justice of Madras, later to be knighted as Judge Advocate General and his brother Frank echoed his father's business success.

Whilst documentary evidence has yet to be found, it is overwhelmingly probable that William Gentle who had qualified as a barrister would have known Alfred Mond who ws also a barrister in the same Inn. That being the case Mond may well have mentioned to Gentle that he was looking for a trustworthy but not necessarily qualified person to 'Watch his back' in his new Swansea constituency and that Gentle recommended the daughter of his wife's sister (My mother).

West Dereham was a village of little more than 400 inhabitants, isolated from the outside world by distance and Fen and despite being little more than a dozen miles from Kings Lynn, which had been the busiest port in Britain, it was a little off the routes to that port. It was in a sense a peripatetic settlement, the homes adjacent to the church were mostly abandoned after the Black Death and replaced by houses built adjacent to the Abbey, whose ruins later became the village's main source of building stone.

Despite its small size it was created market 'town' by King John probably through the influence of Herbert, Archbishop of Canterbury who was born in West

Dereham and had founded the Abbey, which established the village as the epicentre of the sparsely inhabited Hundred of Clackclose. It achieved some vicarious notoriety when Francis Dereham after whose family the village was named, was beheaded for becoming romantically embroiled with Catherine the fifth wife of Henry VIII, surely an unwise step since the matter of Anne Bolyne had shown that the King could turn quite nasty when cuckolded. Not that West Dereham was without some cosmopolitan aspect to its population as a stone in the Churchyard shows.

Emanuel Gaminara. Born Genoa 1794. Died Downham Market 12 December 1892.

As a soldier in the 2nd Imperial Guard under the great Napoleon and also was one of the Grand Army who survived the terrible retreat from Moscow.

Gaminara was apparently taken prisoner at or shortly before Waterloo. On release he settled in West Dereham where he farmed and was a respected (If slightly 'rum') member of the community. My mother as a tiny child remembered him as a customer in her father's shop. His descendant, William Gaminara is a well-known actor.

In 1881, at the time of E. E. Barrow's second marriage, prospects of the village could not have looked better as the Wissey Valley branch railway was being built from Downham Market to Stoke Ferry and West Dereham would have its own station dignified by the name 'Abbey'.

Although the railway would be of great benefit, the village would increasingly lose its 'Stand alone' status and become a satellite of Downham Market. It is interesting that Downham besides reaping the usual benefits when the London – Kings Lynn railway came through in 1847, the town 'About turned'. It ceased to be dependant on Lynn, but could look to Cambridge and London. Oddly this brought little change in character to Downham, which remained an unremarkable country market town. That is until 1942.

That was the year that the opening of RAF Downham Market brought fame and glory to the name as part of 8 (Pathfinder) Group of Bomber Command. Renown and distinction come at a heavy price, almost 200 of its aircraft were lost and more than a thousand men slept their last night on earth in its huts and ate their last meal in its messes Many decorations were awarded to its aircrew including two (sadly posthumous) Victoria Crosses, one to Flight Sergeant Arthur Louis Aaron who, despite mortal wounds made an epic flight in a crippled aircraft to save his crew. There are no yardsticks to measure gallantry, but if there were, surely Flight Sergeant Aaron would stand tall in the most valiant company.

In some measure counterbalancing the losses, 'The Market' being a 'Fog Intensive Dispersal Of' system (Fido) airfield, enabled many aircraft caught out by Fenland fog, possibly damaged and with wounded men on board, to be diverted there to make safe landings. Thus many, many men, whose lives would otherwise have been tragically short, lived long, useful and fulfilled lives.

To revert to family matters, E. E. Barrow had two children by his first wife, Arthur who died in infancy and

Edward Thomas Ebenezer, my mother's half-brother Uncle Ted. Since he moved to Guernsey before I was born I only met him once. A small, gentle man, devoted to photography who had a big job managing a very upmarket St Peter Port, Guernsey, grocery shop. He was a complete contrast to his wife, Mabel (Madge). My mother spoke of the sensation in West Dereham when Ted married the ebullient and stylish Mabel Patching. I recall her as having a big hat and even bigger boobs, brandishing a gold-knobbed stick like a sovereign's sceptre – say what you like, she had Style! Her book of poetry 'Poet's Pie' is still to be found in second-hand bookshops. They had three daughters who were much older than me so their children despite being next generation were my near-contemporaries Gertie, the eldest who married Sid Adams and had one daughter, Maureen, the youngest Moyra married firstly Jack Thompson, (John & Rose) secondly Ronald Crimp (Sandra). The mid daughter Margery was married to Cliff Renouf who despite having been robbed of much schooling by childhood illnesses became a successful businessman. They had four daughters, Barbara, Valerie, Daphne and Pamela, Val died young but not before she had made a mark in Island politics. When Margery lost a leg through illness, Cliff bought her a knitting machine – this machine intended for therapeutic use grew into a large factory operation and many outworkers, producing Guernsey pullovers that sold in the smartest shops worldwide. Unfortunately Margery lost her sight and her health and spent her later years being cared for by her husband.

To come closer to my orbit, E. E. Barrow and Rachel had five children Fred, twins Walter and Elizabeth (my mother), Alice (Nancy as an adult) and Rachel, slightly unusually for the late 19th century all survived.

Fred, the eldest lived in 'Hunnsn' that I later found to be Norfolkspeak for Hunstanton. Cabinetmaker and pillar of the St. John's Ambulance, his upturned and waxed Kaiser Bill moustache being a subject of much pride and care since his admiration of that much-reviled monarch was quite undiminished by his experiences in someplace called 'The War'. His wife, Carrie, my Aunty Tottie, always had a houseful of her 'friends', it being only a matter of the most confidential whisper that they were actually 'paying guests'. It was apparently acceptable to have guests provided they did not pay. Yet when on one occasion some guests left without paying, the incident far from being welcomed as raising the tone of the house, seemed to cause dismay and recriminations. They had a son Jack a few years older than me who after war service, as a Major, became a senior Civil Servant with a wife Mary.

The youngest, Rachel Naylor, 'Tiny' to her siblings, my Aunty Ray was the goggled, gauntleted and breeched, motorcycle riding no nonsense District Nurse. She had no issue but did not object to children, provided they remained inaudible and motionless at all times. Uncle Harry, her elderly husband, had to live under much the same sanction. He was Head Gardener at The Pleasance' a 30 acre garden at Overstrand. Although his wife was said to call a spade a spade, he never handled one, going to work in a suit and supervising his half a dozen minions from an office. They lived in a sort of Grimm's Fairy Tale cottage in the grounds, where on our all too rare visits he would regale me with tales of past triumphs at the Shrewsbury Flower Show. Apparently a head gardener's success at Shrewsbury would bring him discreet offers from other estate owners enabling him to advance his situation. Often the inducement was not entirely tangible, so much as the opportunity to work for an employer of higher rank. Thus a Duke say, could obtain a top man on more modest terms than a mere Viscount!

Despite the distance, we visited both these families, but my mother's twin brother my Uncle Walter and his wife Ethel who kept a butchers shop at Kingswear in Devon were not only never visited but were only spoken of in hushed tones. He had worked with his mother in the West Dereham shop and apparently for a time had a shop of his own near the railway station, whether as a 'branch' or in competition is unclear. I never met either Walter or Ethel since they left for Devon in the late 1920s Officially they left as he needed sea air and since Granny could not manage the shop on her own she sold up but there was certainly more to it than that.

The late 20s would have been a difficult time for village shopkeepers such as Granny. Motorbuses were putting keenly priced 'Company shops' in Downham Market or Kings Lynn within reach. Excursion fares on the railway made the big stores of Cambridge, even London accessible. Thus with a wife and three children, Mollie, Wally and Teddy to feed, while working for a cobweb-pursed mother, must have made life hard for Walter. The event that triggered the departure was undoubtedly the arrival of Peggy, my almost exact contemporary.

Fairly or unfairly, the rest of the family blamed this departure for my Grandmother Rachel's insolvency and move in with my Aunt Nancy. The truth will never be known but my sympathies are with Walter and Ethel.

As regards their family I did in later life meet their eldest child Mollie who married Dutchman Wily Paars whom she had met in the Navy during the war. They farmed in South Africa. I later become friendly with their elder son Wally, as a sergeant in the Coldstream Guards he survived Dunkirk and as a Major in the Devonshire Regiment crossed the Rhine by glider and was briefly a prisoner of war. He became a Colonial Administrator in Kenya and after Independence headed the Police Training College. He met his wife Ann in almost Christopher Robin setting when he was a Guardsman and she was in domestic service in London. They had a daughter Pippa their son John also became an Army Officer.

I also in later life saw something of Walter and Ethel's second son Teddy and his wife Gladys. He was a naval carpenter and afterwards a shop fitter. They had a son John and a daughter Jeanette. Sadly I only once met Walter and Ethel's youngest. Peggy who died young leaving a daughter Jennifer.

The very centre of my childhood experience was with my mother's sister Nancy, her husband Harold Kett and their son Jack, at Wereham some 2 miles from West Dereham. Wereham was slightly larger but more compact than West Dereham. Similarly it had three pubs and two chapels (at daggers drawn) it had a church, but no Vicar, having been demoted to an outstation of West Dereham, a source of some discontent amongst the Derehamites. However it did have a pond invariably known as 'The Pit' an appellation, which the coarser youths prefixed with a short rhyming word. Railed on three sides the fourth being a sort of beach where horses and tumbrels could be washed and wagon wheels tightened in dry weather. Never having had its own Abbey it lacked the provenance of West Dereham, but it did have an outlier – a suburb no less, Flegg Green which was where Aunty Nancy lived and provided a headquarters for that formidable figure Granny, Rachel Barrow. As my sole grandparent, she apparently saw it her duty to be four times as domineering, I don't think I was alone – my mother jumped ship as soon as her father died, but fortunately Nancy could get on with her – whether it was in her nature to be easy going or whether it was an attribute acquired after years of putting up with her husband, Uncle Kett, who in the local patois would have been described as 'cranky'.

From her base camp at Aunty Nancy's Granny be-bagged, be-boxed and widow-weeded circulated like some Flying Dutchman trapped in the Bermuda Triangle, between Hunstanton and Overstrand. For reasons that were concealed from me at the time, she never visited son Walter.

Due to the exigencies of accommodation Granny was

out on circuit when we were at Aunty Nancy's, but she did make occasional forays to us in Swansea, her arrival causing a disturbance redolent of a national disaster. She had a great mistrust of electricity, which was dangerous, gas which would asphyxiate us in our beds, piped water since the Communists had only to put a few drops of poison in the reservoir to kill everyone and indoor sanitation which enabled rats to ascend the pipes and gnaw one's nether regions. Her severest strictures were reserved for Germans who apparently bayoneted babies, and tramcars. Her aversion to the latter stemmed from the firm and sometimes discourteous refusal of conductors to take her to her destination, notwithstanding its being in the opposite direction and remote from the vehicle's tracks. She did not really care for motorcars, but the opportunity to ride in one apparently conferred such a social cachet, that she was prepared to overcome her misgivings. Not that she was a timid person, she quite bravely rode in trains, usually passing the journey, regaling fellow passengers with accounts of past rail disasters, citing excerpts from Mcgonagal's poem about the 'terrible happenings on the silv'ry Tay' to illustrate her points. I believe she was not averse to travelling by omnibus, provided she was seated near enough to the front to call out advice to the driver.

It was years before I discovered that grandmothers were not necessarily evil-tempered, obtuse and clad in ground-length apparel and smelt of lavender and wee-wee. What my granny, or indeed myself at that time, would have made of grannies, great-grannies even, wearing trousers, driving cars and generally part of society rather than just critics of it, I cannot imagine.

Besides the pilgrimages to Norfolk, I do have very distant memories of other but brief trips, possibly long weekends, to London, Bristol and even one to Holland, but 'Going away' meant going to Aunty Nancy's which we did at some Easters but always every summer. In my case after the age of 10 when I could be sent on ahead parcel-like so could spend the entire school summer holidays there. Hence of all my uncles and aunties both real and honorary, Aunty Nancy made the greatest impact on me and the times spent there loomed and still loom large on my consciousness.

11

Aunty Nancy's

It never rained at Aunty Nancy's, no one told you to stop what you were doing at Aunty Nancy's, no one made you wash when you weren't dirty at Aunty Nancy's, no one made a fuss if you got your clothes messy. Neither time nor circumstance seemed to be governed by the rigid rules of the adult world, besides which, there was the excitement of discovery, since in and out and around, there were limitless opportunities for expeditions and searches.

The excitement of the trip started with the packing of the TRUNK, the big black cavernous object with its leather straps and copious buckles, packed and re packed ready to be heaved and hefted to the huge Albion lorry by the 'Luggage in Advance' men. Then, after an excited, sleepless night, the DAY with the big brown shiny suitcases and the black hatbox, one waited in the hall for the taxi.

Then the TRAIN, the long haul to Paddington, the interminable fields, the telegraph wires dipping and rising as the poles flashed past, the towns, cars seen on roads, cows in meadows, houses, clumps of trees. In towns, the back gardens with sheds revealing their tatty secrets, the level crossings' impatient queues the coal yards, and all the time the clackedy-clack, clackerdy–clack of the rails. And, the prize of all the Hall's

Distemper cut-out white coasted giants carrying their ladder-like sign.

At bustling stations, the gradually approaching ringing blows of the wheel-tapper and, stretching up with face hard against the corridor window, seeing his shiny black hat pass below.

The sudden darkness and change of noise of the tunnels, everything in the compartment seen reflected in the dark windows, the flashes of the platelayers' lamps, the sulphurous smell. The startling thunder and the throbbing, the flashing lights of a train going the other way.

The dazzling bursting into sunshine, the dining car, the cutlery jingling, the steward swaying as he noted the order on his pad. The highpoint of the meal, when he brought round the biscuits in the tin with the train on it, the engine on one side and the carriages stretching around the other three sides. The steam and engines at Swindon and vast workshops with lights and fires glimpsed, the Huntley & Palmers sign at Reading, the factories' uncomfortable jumbles, the His Master's Voice sign, the big gasometers, the slowing past the vast sidings, the first glimpse of an electric train, coal wagons, lorries, then the slowing down and the creep into the dinginess of Paddington

The scuttle and panic of getting a taxi, mother's enjoiners to 'be careful that he doesn't overcharge us, he doesn't look honest to me'. This delivered in the piercing tones that only the hard of hearing seem to achieve. One could only cringe and hope the cabbie suffered from the same affliction.

The excitement of the streets, the traffic, the red buses with 'General' written on the side, rushing and bustle, people so close you could touch them, a gold hunter watch urgently consulted, anxiety about the 'connection', and the anxiety as the meter clicked in three-penny jumps, 'look it's three shillings and we're still miles away, whatever you do Tom don't pay him more than three and six'.

The smoky halls of Liverpool Street, the anxious search for the Lynn train and the gentle journey, with its inevitable litany of Audley End, Bishop's Stortford, Cambridge, Ely, Littleport and, finally and dozily, Downham Market. Downham had no over bridge so down train passengers had to fearfully cross the tracks in front of that monstrous locomotive, breathing smoke and spitting steam, and hissing like a fire-eating dragon impatient to leap forward and crush you under its gigantic iron wheels. All the time, the bustling anxiety lest anything had been left behind and the possibility that Wade's man had forgotten to turn up. Then the luggage had to be safely stowed in the car and finally the sleepy dazed frayed arrival at Aunty Nancy's.

What one remembers is the smell, not the faint polishy all pervading odour of home but different smells in every room of which there were several on the ground floor. There was the living room where everything seemed to take place. It had a big, never cleared table, some higgledy-piggledy newspaper-strewn chairs and squeezed into one corner an ancient be-sconced upright piano. This room smelt of fires and oil lamps and cats and a dozen other things but mainly it smelt of Uncle Kett. The smell in no way reflected any reluctance to use the scant washing facilities of a bowl in the kitchen and water from a kettle balanced on the living room fire, but was a delicious cocktail of paint and wood shavings and 4d per ounce shag tobacco, smoked in a pipe with the stem so bitten that the bowl threatened his 'Old Bill' moustache. Uncle Kett did have a given name, but no one used it, perhaps few knew it. He would have liked to be called Mister Kett, but to almost all, including his wife he was just plain unadorned Kett. The vicar called him Mister Kett, but that unfortunate cleric's well meant token of respect was taken as condescension. Uncle Kett addressed him as Mister Parson although addressing him was something he tended to avoid.

On the opposite side of the little dark hallway was the Drawing Room which in contrast to the rest of the stone-flagged downstairs had a wooden floor and an exiguous square of carpet with green, silk, not-to-be-sat-on chairs and an ormolu clock that pinged the hours, with a rude lady under a glass dome. Other than when a cat had accidentally been shut in, it had a fustiness all of its own.

Behind the living room and down a step was the kitchen, which smelt of cooking, washing, well water and cats.

The big slate-slabbed larder just smelt of cats – no wonder there were up to six of them. There were two big ones, Fluffy and Highleg, proud and independent, black as a vicar's hat, which to my delight chased each other along the piano keys. They were joined by a marmalade called Typhus, scourge of cats, dogs, humans and for all

I know horses, yet even when I was too small to lift him would allow me to drag him around like a rag doll. My favourite was Megrim a once black now threadbare brown, that kept having kittens, most of which mysteriously disappeared, reputedly adopted by fairies, but some were kept such as the exquisite Topsy and the wily Wrytail. Megrim would purr and cuddle, cuddle and purr and with Uncle Kett's connivance, lick the butter off my bread.

On the right, atop the dizzily steep, threadbare-carpeted stairs, was Uncle and Aunt's room, opposite was Granny's room, vacated by her of course but still with her redolence, where my parents slept. There was a marble-topped washstand with jug, basin and matching soap dish and a pair of chamber pots. The bed was vast with a huge tester canopy, whose patterned hangings conspired with the dancing candle flame to create terrifying hobgoblins and beasties. I slept in this room shoehorned into a cot which got smaller with each visit, until I was promoted to a mattress on the landing floor.

Straight ahead from the top of the stairs, accessed by a hatchway was the spider-ridden attic of the lean-to kitchen, where cousin Jack slept under the rafters.

The best smells were in the Shed. It was the source of Uncle Kett's paint and wood shavings aroma, but so much else besides, turpentine, linseed oil, creosote, and a hundred unnameable scents. Here Kett plied his trade.

This trade was nominally that of wheelwright, but how much of a wheel he could wright was open to question. As I recall he did not have the gear to shape and bore the great oak hubs of wagon and tumbrel wheels, and probably did not have the skill to cut the spoke-mortises delicately angled so that the spokes were exactly evenly spaced and would give the wheel its shock-absorbing dish. He could undoubtedly make a replacement for a rotted spoke, using a sound one as a pattern from which to fashion the ash, and I suppose it is possible that he could reproduce an elm felloe. There were occasionally tumbrels or even wagons in the yard but I suspect that this would have been for some small body repair or for painting.

The shed was used for general carpentry and involved exciting things such as the grindstone, the big vice and tools like the yard-long mahogany try-plane. The floor was soft underfoot, bare earth with a carpet of sawdust. It was an obstacle course of half finished jobs. Some were customer's work, a wagon wheel needing a spoke, a barrow with a broken handle, a partly tine-less hay rake, a chair with a broken leg, all undoubtedly long past the date when they would 'definitely be ready'. Any customer remonstrating about an item weeks overdue would be indignantly made aware that 'A proper job took time'. Besides these, there were the really important jobs – yet another bird table to join the dozens of others in the garden jungle, or a weather vane or a little windmill that one day might augment the many that sprouted from every prominence. Then there was 'Billy's Shed'. Billy was presumably a one-time helper, but the name had a lost-in-the-mists-of-time aura like Walter's Road or Padley's Yard, or for that delight of schoolboys, Buckler's Hard. Nothing much went on in Billy's shed, the bicycles were kept there, magnificent upright machines, Ladies bicycles with broken skirt-guard strings, bicycles inexpertly painted in strange colours. Rusting spokes, flat tyres, peeling plating abounded but not on one huge black, copiously oiled machine, sadly anonymous, its make being lost under multiple layers of paint – Uncle Kett's personal transport. The shiningly plated lamp of this veritable Bentley of a bicycle had its own special shelf in the living room, where it stood like some prized trophy. Its taking down, meticulous cleaning and filling with water and pungent carbide, which preceded an excursion to the Chequers, had all the solemnity of a religious rite. The lamp bore the legend 'Lucas, King of the Road', a most appropriate appellation since Kett himself as trilby hatted and trouser clipped, he proceeded on his machine with regal majesty.

Billy's shed had an exciting upstairs where 'The Oak' was kept, stock-in-trade for Kett's secondary occupation – coffin maker. Magnificent slabs of oak, some chalked with the names of intended clients. It being Uncle Kett's custom to approach elderly (and not so elderly) neighbours with a fulsome account of a fine lot of oak 'just come in', and a pressing plea to be allowed to 'put some one side, ready for when the time comes'. Since money up front was involved, this must have done wonders for Uncle Kett's meagre cash flow. Unkind villagers made scurrilous suggestions that the same timber was the subject of more than one transaction. I cannot believe this to have been true, although reports of customers being in ill health did seem to cause great anxiety to Uncle Kett.

There was also another structure, never referred to by any name as I recall, but whose smell in summer heat announced its function. A dreadful place where spiders lurked and beetles crawled and flies insistently buzzed. Fascinatingly it was a two holer, although the sociable possibilities were never, as far as I am aware, invoked

Then there was The Well, to be kept away from, how I envied cousin Jack, a big boy, being allowed to crank its creaking handle and wind its rusty, complaining chain. Washing water came from The Butt, but the deliciously aromatic galvanised buckets of drinking water came from The Well. What a delight it was to be allowed, firmly held, to peer down and watch the bucket being lowered, canting on its side as it struck the circle of sky reflected in the water and glugged towards the bottomless depths.

I have to admit that at times I hated Jack, he was always held up as an example of cleverness – but he was seven years older than me – it is I who should have been praised for being nearly as clever as he was! Jack was good at 'Sports', why it should be considered so praiseworthy to be able to run faster and jump higher than everyone else I did not (And still do not) know. After all, if you want to go fast get a motorbike, if you want to get up higher get a ladder. Moreover I was brought up to regard mud, dirty water and creepy crawlies as things to be avoided; yet he was praised for mucking about in ditches and putting names to all the bugs and insects.

Then there was The Orchard. A near impenetrable expanse of brambles and nettles not, as I recall, with many, or indeed any, fruit trees extant.

At the far end were the hutches, where if a grown up was on hand to hold back the brambles and nettles, The Bunnies could be visited. The purpose of these animals was unclear, for if rabbit was on the menu, there were always assurances that it was not one of The Bunnies. Occasionally Uncle Kett would busy himself making travelling hutches in which rabbits were dispatched on the roof of the weekly motorbus, allegedly for their 'holidays'.

Then there was Toby, a dog the colour of a lion, the size of a lion and with the disposition of a lion with hemorrhoids. It lived in a kennel to which it was attached by a chain strong enough to anchor a battleship. It devoted itself to barking and defecating. It was fed by Uncle Kett casting bones or dog biscuits from a point well out of reach of the dripping, growling, gnashing jaws. Watering was more of a problem. This involved throwing a stick so it landed just beyond the dog's radius of action whilst a swift intrepid dash was made to swap drinking bowls. The stick needed to land just out of the dog's reach. Too far and the beast would immediately abandon any attempt to reach it, too near he could in a flash pick it up. In either case having time to attack Uncle Kett before he could leap clear. Added to which there was the ever-present possibility of slipping on the dog mess in the danger area.

Just why he kept such a dog was unknown, Kett did hint that it was because, 'You never know.' Admittedly with a shedful of tools and valuable timber a guard dog was advisable, but it would be a very foolish intruder who ventured into the no-go area defined by Toby's chain and a bark was no danger signal since the beast barked all the time. I do not recall Toby being taken for walks but I believe that Uncle Kett did so in the very early morning whilst the dog's reflexes were still deadened by sleep and the road was clear both of neighbours and livestock.

If Uncle Kett did go out walking, in the evenings say, he would invariably take The Gun. This ancient weapon with intriguing little hammers on either side of the breech leant against the living room wall just inside the door, where it was said to be 'handy if needed in a hurry'. Again what sort of circumstance would give rise to a hurried need was never made clear, particularly as cartridges were never in evidence. Also unclear was why this cartridgeless gun had to be carried on walks, as was indeed the purpose of Uncle Kett's walks. They were never to the pub since although it was only a couple of hundred yards distant; it was always visited by bicycle, presumably to distinguish him from lesser, bicycleless drinkers.

I assume The Gun was carried as a token of rank, like a municipal mace, after all a man striding purposefully, with a gun under his arm was undoubtedly a person of some consequence, an occupier, even possibly an owner of, land that needed to be protected from vermin and thieves. Furthermore having the right to bear arms was redolent of the upper ranks of chivalry, never mind that that right could be purchased at any Post Office for five shillings.

Uncle Kett was far removed from such upper echelons, but as a self-employed master craftsman he did enjoy a standing above that of the ordinary villagers. Furthermore owning a pair of modest cottages next door, whose weekly rents of a shilling or so must have appreciably augmented the family income and placed him as a Man of Property at least on a par with the more respectable smallholders and shopkeepers, and nudging the status of the publicans.

Aunty Nancy possibly enjoyed higher standing than her husband, mainly due to her Women's Institute activities. Not that she was President or anything, but apparently her seniority and regular attendance gained her a sort of elder statesman position in what was after all the mainstay of village society. She was also the icer of cakes. For the cost of the ingredients plus a modest percentage, she would appropriately embellish a cake, whenever a wedding or baptism was in the offing.

Aunty Nancy's was a little way out of the village, the visiting of which was something of an expedition. It was, as I would later discover like Gaul, divided into three parts Front Street, which embraced the church, the pond and the houses around them and was where the best people lived. Back Street was a less prestigious address, but definitely a cut above the Council houses of Top End.

Front Street was a main road full of exciting traffic, wagons, tumbrels, motor lorries, steam carts and cars, Morris's, Austins, Singers and Fords. But the source of the most exciting cars was the Manor, at weekends Humbers, Lea Francis's, Daimlers even, it was said a

Rolls Royce, were among their visitors. Some of whom it was rumoured were from London, which according to the yellow AA sign on the barn at the start of the village was 84 miles distant. The Manor cars were driven with panache not manifest in the more local motorists. Appropriately they were known as the 'fast set'.

The Manor itself was a brick building with lots of windows on three floors. Clearly visible from the road but invariably without sign of life. The owner was rarely seen, being, so it was said, in business in London. He was occasionally glimpsed speeding past in his Armstrong Sidderley with his wife at the wheel. His failure to employ a chauffeur marked him out as not being real gentry, and certainly not a proper squire, and the fact that his wife drove a motorcar cast some doubt on her status as a lady. Matters got worse when the Manor passed to a Baronet. Spoken of as belonging to an old Norfolk family made me imagine all his relatives were elderly, but the only known certainty was that he owned an aeroplane, which he kept at Marham, the recently opened RAF airfield. This placed him high in my admiration, but the rumour was that his wife flew it, which in no way impugned her status since the Duchess of Bedford was a well-know aviatrix. It all seemed an extraordinary state of affairs since I was quite sure that if I ever had an aeroplane and also the rather less desirable accoutrement, a wife; I was sure that I would not allow the latter to fly the former – a prediction that time would eventually prove to be incorrect. The machine was probably a Gypsy Moth. This 2-seater, open cockpit biplane was a very popular aircraft not from any technical or economic reasons but because it was then the only machine in its class with a locker sufficiently commodious to accommodate a golf-bag.

Back street was much quieter, the blacksmith and the butcher presided over a terrace of modest dwellings. As relatives of a Master Craftsman, one clearly did not visit Top End.

Since there was no squire, or at least not one in permanent residence, no doctor, and the vicarage was in the next village, the chief citizen, by default should have been the schoolmaster. I have forgotten his name and have no recollection of what he looked like, but I do recall the opprobrium that he attracted by keeping poultry. Everyone kept chickens, some ducks, and geese even, but to have meetings chaired, concerts presided over and fetes opened, by a person who not only kept poultry in excessive numbers but also described himself as a poultry farmer, was scarcely acceptable. Had he been a real farmer, it would have been different. Farmers kept cows and pigs had horses and grew crops and were undoubted men of substance; they dressed the part, they looked the part, they enjoyed respect and were far removed from a person with a shedful of chickens.

This left a vacancy as it were for the 'top job'. There were several farmers who were potential candidates. The front-runner was undoubtedly one named Churchill. Whilst his namesake had yet to achieve his later eminence, his was nevertheless a name commanding respect, and his Christian name; Willoughby had a ring of authority. The aura was heightened by his somewhat ample figure; his weighty pronouncements on world affairs and his ownership of a tractor, set him apart from lesser agriculturists. These included the Carters whose holding was pathetically small, but having a thoroughfare, Carter's Lane, named after them bestowed a certain cachet. Although an acre or two did guarantee standing, it was possible for the landless to achieve some status, the Grimes' provided kennelling where greyhounds could be lodged in anonymity safe from nobblers so were obviously persons in whom trust could be placed. Mr Impson an otherwise unremarkable person was propelled to prominence when he became a civilian tanker driver, responsible for fuelling the mighty Handley Page bombers at Marham airfield, thus enjoying the respect due to any Civil Servant. Kett's credentials as a master craftsman were somewhat esoterically reinforced by his claim of direct descent from Edward Kett who was hanged from the tower of Wyndham Church in 1549.

12

Solving Mysteries

There were a number of shopkeepers in Wereham, the leading one being Mr. Winter whose shop, on Front Street of course, was a magnificent emporium, excitingly dark, redolent of exotic comestibles beyond the purse of ordinary folk, and where, in Mr. Winter's estimation, it was a privilege to be allowed to deal.

A step below Winter's was Howlett's, who whilst as a shop was but a shadow of Winter's, it did enjoy the cachet of being kept by the Postmaster, who representing King George himself, stood high in the village pecking order.

There were other shops such as Handslip's, mostly small part time establishments, which sought to capture business with the variety and garishness of the sweets, which they stocked. As the wife of a tradesman who depended on the goodwill of the village, Aunty Nancy had to spread her custom, which meant that her trade was spread very thinly indeed. It was not apparent at the time but later I was to realise that any paper money other than perhaps a ten-shilling note would have been a stranger to her purse.

There was no baker in the village. Bread was brought round house to house in a green van by a smilingly genial man in knee breeches, grown-ups called him Baker, and in deference to his adult status I called him Mr. Baker.

His capacious basket not only carried Tins, Cobs, Browns and Milks, but also Cakes. Mr. Baker's cakes were not the effete éclairs and meringues of the town shops but great icing-topped buns that a childish fist could scarcely grasp and jam puffs, mighty triangles of pastry oozing a chin-dribbling abundance of raspberry jam. Occasionally after Mr. Baker had pointedly discussed at length how much 'the young gentleman' liked his cakes, one or the other would be purchased.

The doyen of village trade was Bramwell Box, the blacksmith, tall as a tree and patriotically bearded. Later as I was taught something of the Old Testament prophets and the references in Job to 'The sparks fly upward' and 'Sparks of fire leap out', it was Bramwell Box that filled my mind's eye. His smithy was a vast cavern, black as a deacon's hat, its recesses rhythmically illuminated as the forge flame flared in response to each stroke of the bellows. Pulsatingly discernable like some satanic acolyte in the furnace glow, was 'The Lad', who doubled as a blower and a striker. Although the smith undertook a wide range of tasks, it was rare to pass without there being at least one mighty Shire horse tethered outside, its hooves ringing impatiently on the cobbles, whilst inside the anvil rang as Bramwell shaped a glowing shoe. Shortly he would emerge, the shoe on tongs and would lift and hold a great hoof between his knees and apply the shoe with sizzle and smoke, and a quite unforgettable smell. When nailing, the mouthful of mustads, would be driven home too quickly for the eye to follow.

The Smithy was a public place, but never more so

than when a cartwheel was to be re-tyred. With the help of the more able-bodied onlookers, the wheel, a hefty piece of kit especially if it was from a tumbrel, was positioned on the tyre plate, a five-feet diameter circle of iron let into the cobbled forecourt. Box would appear with his blower/striker in acolyte-like attendance and having acknowledged his audience, would set to work.

A few full arm sledgehammer blows would sever the worn iron tyre and send it clanging clear, provoking a collective gasp of approval, reminiscent of tricoteuses at a guillotining. If the wheel was well made it would remain intact, otherwise the felloes would part company from the spokes, some of which would in turn, sag away from the hub, leaving a pile of firewood at Box's feet, giving rise to expressions of derision, (and slanderous comments that the wheel must have been a Kett job).

The Box-Kett relationship whilst mutually interdependent was not a cordial one. If a wheel collapsed due to the loss of a tyre-hoop then there would be acrimonious debate as to whether the workmanship of wheel or tyre was to blame. Of course as often as not it would have occurred on a hot day and be due to the carter failing to keep the wheels wet by backing into the village pond.

In the meantime the new tyre, a strip of steel, which had been bent in a little roller machine and hammer-welded to a size carefully measured with chalk and string, would have been heating since early morning. Too big for the forge, it had to be buried in a circle of glowing coke on the forecourt, quietly approaching incandescence being turned and turned again until its whole circumference glowed brightly.

Bramwell and the boy, each tong-equipped, would reverently lift it from the pyre and drop it over the wheel that awaited it on the tyreing plate. There would be smoke and the tang of scorched wood, immediately followed by a great fog of steam as buckets of water were tipped over it.

The show over, the audience might disperse or perhaps drift across the road to peer through the window at the butcher, wielding his cleaver, splitting ribs a hair's breadth from his fingers. He was called Margeson. No one seemed to have proper names like Jones or Thomas but were exotically identified by names such as Gathercole, Gotobed and Holdgate.

Commerce was dominated by Mr. Yallop who kept the George and Dragon, Like Kett his Christian name was not in common currency, he was addressed as Yallop or Mr. Yallop according to the addressor's relative status, but rude urchins awed by Mrs Yallop's commanding appearance would (behind his back) call him George. Cars were repaired in the yard behind the pub; petrol was dispensed at the front from a hose on an arm hinged to the pub wall, fed by a hand-cranked pump. Filling up a car always was a crowd puller. The cover of the pump was unlocked and slid back revealing the mechanism. The hinged arm would be swung out and the nozzle of the hose would be inserted into the appropriate orifice in the vehicle. The handle would be turned slowly and deliberately, three and bit times until it met a stop, which indicted that a meticulously measured gallon had been delivered. Then the handle would be rapidly unwound ready to part with a second gallon of 'Motor Spirit'. Just occasionally a third gallon was required, but this was a rare enough event to provoke comment while a fourth gallons was enough to bring drinkers out from the bar. The process was completed by the hose being shaken and massaged to extract the last drop of the precious fluid.

There was a Shell glass dome on the pump, the enamelled sign said B.P., but it was widely believed that the fuel was actually some inferior product such as R.O.P. This Russian Oil Products fuel came out at 11d (4½p) per gallon as against the 1/2d (6p) for the cheapest 'Commercial' grade from the major producers such as 'Pratt's', 'Regent' or 'Cleveland'. Undoubtedly subsidised by a hard-currency hungry USSR, to admit to buying ROP was to court social ostracism.

Mr. Yallop drove a Ford Model A, towing a trailer in pursuance of his other manifold business interests the most prominent being selling water from milk churns filled at the village well. It was called a well but it was in fact just a spout from which a stream of ice-cold water emerged. Although allegedly unfailing, in summer the flow decreased to a trickle, making Yallop's monopolising of the spout seriously unpopular. He drew his clientele from those outlying dwellings too poor to have a well or whose fenland location made such a convenience impracticable.

Yallop also collected, charged and delivered accumulators for those sufficiently affluent to own a wireless set. He also dealt in second-hand furniture and indeed in anything from which a profit might be made.

The bar trade he drew from Back Street; there was another pub, the Nag's Head, that catered for Top End, and the Chequers, which drew its trade from the more outlying residents. Persons living in Front Street did not of course visit public houses.

Yallop's old Model A Ford, apart from its other duties, also served as the village taxi. Whilst the 3/6 (17.5p) charged for the 5-mile trip to town was not unreasonable, few could afford this other than in dire emergency. I seem to recall that he had no telephone and one contacted him by ringing the telephone box just outside, something that called for some persistence if illness say, required transport in the smaller hours of the night. I seem to recall on Village Fete days, a Ford, possibly Yallop's, powering the greyhound racing 'Hare'. Parked at one end of a field, one rear corner would be jacked up, the wheel removed and replaced by a drum this would rapidly wind in a rope attached to a rag-stuffed rabbit-skin 'hare' from the far end of the field. This would be pursued by a pack of barking 'greyhounds' of assorted and indeterminate breeds. The car itself would serve as a betting shop.

Everyone in the country spoke in a funny way; they seemed to start the word off long then cut it off. I could make out when someone wanted some *waaatr* from the well and *buuur* was what you spread on bread, but it was years before I realised that the place they called *Swaaarfm* was in fact Swaffham. Why they should all talk in this extraordinary way was a total mystery. Although I came from an Anglicised and had it rammed into me that to 'talk Welshy' was 'common', my accent must have seemed equally strange.

Then there were the words the children used, the horses did not make manure as they did at home, they shat. The just barely acceptable 'bum' gave way to 'arse', even the girls used this most extreme of obscenities. Of course here the girls were not like those at home, silly, stuck up and generally pretty useless, they were more like boys. The likes of Dorothy Grimes and Lorna Hayhoe played cricket, threw stones, built dens and climbed trees. Although they were sometimes prepared to adjudicate, they would never participate in contests for height or distance. Assembling data from various sources established that this refusal was not due simply to a spoilsport attitude but due to a serious defect in female architecture.

This brought up the long-standing speculation as to the difference between girls and boys. O K women had busts and long hair, girls did not have the former and anyway girl babies' hair was as short as boy babies. There must be some other difference, otherwise how would parents know whether to give them a boy's or a girl's name? Presumably it was in the area always strictly concealed. It had also been inferred that this difference was in some way connected with the arrival of those babies, but the exact nature of it remained obscure. Any enquiry was met by the all purpose reply 'You'll understand when you're older'.

Although the stork and gooseberry bush theorems of

infant arrival were clung to in some quarters, the mummies' tummies hypothesis gained general acceptance but this left unexplained how they got there. Some of the coarser boys alleged a most improbable procedure.

'Busts' were a further source of mystery not the physical characteristics, their shape was obvious and statuary took care of the fine detail, but not their purpose. I had (Shock, horror) seen the end of one put in a baby's mouth, but this seemed a slovenly practice by women too poor or to idle to buy a proper dummy.

Whilst statuary made the upper parts clear, neither it nor any other source provided any clue to the 'Down below'. On the rare occasions when the drapery was indiscreet, the gentlemen statues had a willie, but lady statues had nothing. Much the same was true of paintings in art galleries. Rare and treasured literature such as 'Health and Efficiency' was even less helpful, as both sexes were photographed with a leg tantalisingly obscuring the one bit one needed to see.

On balance of probabilities, girls definitely had something there; some boys even had words for it, words that were even ruder than arse. But even those boys with a number of alternative names for it, seemed as ignorant as I as to its precise form.

Then at a stroke knowledge took a quantum leap.

During a late night, hushed-voiced family conference at Aunty Nancy's the word 'Ladymansbill' was overheard. At first it was dismissed as being a word like Mortgage (whatever that was), which belonged to the alien adult world. Yet it was whispered in a way redolent of shame and dark secrecy, as indeed mortgage sometimes was. When subsequent enquiry was met with a shocked and embarrassed, 'You'll understand when you're older', it seemed obvious that it had to do with the source of babies. Thus, in a flash it dawned on me, on the reasonable premise that a woman was a 'lady man' and connecting 'Bill' and 'Willie' made it obvious that a Ladymansbill was what girls had down there. This attractive theory was in due course superseded, but it was to be many, many years before an older cousin explained the actual meaning of this word to me.

I had deduced that Granny had kept a shop, a fact that seemed so wrapped in shame an evasion that had I been sentient of such matters might have concluded to be a 'House of ill repute'. I was later to discover that it was the Post Office in the next village, West Dereham and that the opprobrium arose from the fact that she had ceased trading unable to meet her commitments to suppliers. As has been said, this defalcation was alleged to have been precipitated by her son Walter's departure. The rights and wrongs of this we do not know but there was a rift and my mother never again saw her twin brother.

The rest of the family (which in practical terms meant my father) had shouldered the burden of her debts and over years was gradually paying them off. The largest and most serious sum apparently being the account owed to a Messrs Ladyman & Co, a Kings Lynn wholesaler.

13

IT

For some time now the letters I T have presaged surfeit of information, in those yonder times IT was an euphemism for that sniggeringly whispered word S**, or put another way, an infuriating lack of information. To sisterless boys, girls were an alien species and even speaking to them was as wicked as smoking or stealing sweets from Woolworth's. It is different now, for half a century my old school has been in purpose-designed, (i.e. jerry built and unsuitable) premises and although it has been transmogrified into unisex 'Bishop Gore' its fame is no longer Episcopally based but rests on Dylan Thomas having been an alumnus, but as I understand it, his leaving some half a dozen years before my arrival, had been welcomed by staff and pupils alike. I am sure that the 17th century worthy would be less dismayed to find himself displaced by poet more remembered for his thirst than his verse, as he would be to find that girls are admitted.

In my day such mysterious creatures were educated in segregated purdah. Decades later when entering an erstwhile girls' school that had been put to other use, I half-expected to be ejected by hockey-stick wielding amazons. Even when boys' schools and girls' schools shared premises, solid walls divided the two halves and the respective entrances were liable to be in different streets. This modern unisex approach to education would, one imagines give ultra-bike shed opportunities well beyond the shared Woodbine, but then with all the kids being ferried to school in 4x4s, there is presumably no bike shed.

Although one travelled on the tram with girls, there was little opportunity to even speak to them since they tended to travel *laagered* in giggling, defensive huddles. Acquaintance with boys with sisters was eagerly sought, for although direct information was sparse, snippets could be assembled piece by piece to provide some insight into female physiognomy.

Whilst 'Health and Efficiency' remained a much sought-after standard work, it provided great titillation (an unfortunate word perhaps) but little information; more could be gained by inference and innuendo, from the 'Razzle', a sort of saucy postcard humorous magazine. Today's 'Top Shelf' publications would have been riches beyond our wildest dreams. The idea that the depictions and descriptions in full cinematic Technicolor glory would one day be beamed into every house, would have been quite outside our ken. For us in those unenlightened times, the most fruitful source of visual information remained the walls of the more insalubrious type of public lavatory.

It had become firmly established that some sort of mutual activity was called for although who did what to who was the subject of heated debate. When a woman teacher left to get married (There were no married women teachers) speculation rose to fever pitch. There was one boy who did put forward a description that was had we known it, totally accurate, but this scenario seemed so far-fetched that it was dismissed out of hand.

Eventually various influences moved the jigsaw towards completion, but there was a further enigma. Although 'It' was obviously a fairly widespread grown-up thing, there were few grown ups one could imagine engaging in that sort of activity, one's parents for starters. Presumably they had done it at least once, but what about the vicar? He had four children so must have done it four times – not at all the sort of thing that was expected of a parson. What about the King and Queen, they had four sons and a daughter? One could not really imagine Queen Mary even knowing about anything so disgusting. In fact it was difficult to imagine any of the Royal Family even going to the lavatory, enquiry on that matter was met with such horror that one had to conclude that they did not.

There existed one place where allegedly this procedure could be witnessed – Singleton Park. A thick belt of woods lined its high stone eastern boundary wall and it was strongly rumoured that couples went there to 'do it' and the thick undergrowth would enable them to be observed. All one needed to do was to follow any couple who venture across the grass towards the trees. One did see couples strolling with encircling arms, some pausing for a mutual tonsil-licking session, but always rather than dashing for cover, they would continue their hip-to-hip stroll. Had they not done so, I am sure all of us were too afraid of the Parkee to walk on his precious grass.

Some boys recommended sand dunes as a better

observation location and indeed some claimed 'Hundreds' of sightings, but their description of the activity was so vague as to call their veracity into question. In an case all thought of this activity, which in of the argot of the day was called 'pimping', was brought to an abrupt halt by a newspaper report that some vicious thieves were to 'Get the cat'. It was found that instead of this being a rather nice reward reminiscent of getting a kitten for Christmas that it was a whipping so barbarous that it was reserved for violent robbers and pimps.

The sister of one boy seemed to be such a mine of information that first hand experience was suspected but inconsistencies eventually revealed that she was imaginatively extrapolating information gleaned from covert consultation of her father's cache of 'Razzle' magazines.

Soon after a broad appreciation of matters had been established came the knowledge that actions did not necessarily have consequences – this breakthrough being originated by the discovery of a mysterious object in, of all places, the Fives Court. At first thought to be some kind of jellyfish, an older boy immediately identified it as a 'Frenchie'. The form swot said it was a 'Birth Controller' although the parturative connection remained unexplained. Eventually the exact use and function of such devices was deduced and it was alleged that they were readily obtainable at Dirty Black's, a well-known fancy goods shop.

This knowledge seemed to open up vast possibilities, removing as it did girls' chief objection to experimentation. However enthusiasm was dampened by the rumour that by law the manufacturers had to ensure that a certain percentage had invisible holes in them. This apparently had something to do with maintaining the birth rate to protect the Empire, a difficult concept for us to grasp since to us the Empire was the music hall theatre, and to confuse matters further Dirty Black's shop adjoined the stage door. Eventually it was assumed that this location was chosen because actors and actresses did it all the time.

All this as against a background of the oft-repeated mantra the 'Girls can lead you astray'. This tied up with the popular assertion that they were all 'Dying for it'. Indeed there were debates as to whether this yearning was more likely to be found in the High School or Glanmor or, in a more mature age group, Woolworth or Marks and Spencer.

This was all manifestly untrue and that one needed to, as the marketing men now say, 'Create a Demand'. Scratching a palm, or touching an earlobe, seemed to create more annoyance than compliance. A 'French kiss' was said to be extremely effective, but even if contact could be achieved, inserting one's tongue between reluctant teeth seemed unwise.

The cinema would seem to provide the best ambience but since 'Meet you inside' was not an option, two tickets had to be bought, and even then there was no guarantee that back row seats would be available. Furthermore a cheaper establishment such as the Carlton or the Rialto was unacceptable, the Plaza or Albert Hall being invariably demanded, although the double seats of the latter did have unique advantages. These however were negated by the ease with which a sharp dig in the ribs could be delivered should bounds be overstepped. An ever-present problem was the usherette's torch that was shone along the row to ensure that all heads were facing forward and that there were two hands on every lap.

What is today called 'Alternative orientation' was the subject of sniggering jokes but I certainly never encountered it. I was shocked to learn years later that one lad with whom I had been quite friendly was (or perhaps had become), homosexual. At least one master was supposed to have such inclinations, but this seems to have been because he was a bachelor with a slightly sinister manner.

There was one freelance teacher, a self-styled a 'Professor of Music' no less, who did commit mild indecent assaults but a vigorous kick in the shins ensured a permanent cessation of such improprieties seemingly without bad feelings on either side. I imagine that this was more satisfying, and probably more successful than a tiresome recourse to law. In the case of this person such retaliation was particularly effective since as a wearer of knickerbockers his bestockinged shins were especially vulnerable.

Not that we only thought about sex, although our expanding knowledge made it difficult not to, even in school. Double meanings seemed to abound in 'Agony' Lewis's attempts to introduce us to literature – even when Shakespeare was appropriately Bowdlerised – Lady Macbeth's wish to have her access stopped seemed hilarious and even the Lady of Shallot could raise a snigger. 'Christie Barrett' the toffee-chewing history master had only to refer to a period in history to reduce the form to guffaws. I sometimes wondered if these lapses were always unintended, certainly 'Wee Willy' Wilcox's Spoonerisation of his enjoiner to bring our stools and textbooks to the front of the chemistry class, cannot have been accidental.

I do not wish to give the impression that all adolescent boys were obsessed with sex, it is just that I did not knowingly meet any that were not, but in fairness even the most priapic had other interests, such as batting averages and football league tables, collecting bird's eggs or, for that matter tiddldeywinks. However there was one other activity that united all boys and possibly even girls in common cause – cigarettes.

I do not mean the furtive, sick-making cough and spit shared Woodbine, but the much moiré constructive aspect – cigarette cards.

There was a bewildering array of brands. The basic article for the workman and the scholar was the Woodbine sold in packets of 5 for 2d (about 1p), bought singly by the desperately doshless at a half-penny (¼p). These were of only limited interest since they could only be smoked since they did not include cards.

Gentlemen of discernment smoked Gold Flake and macho types smoked Capstan. Craven A showed an independence of thought. State Express or Kensitas made a man stand out in a crowd. Such brands as Abdula that cost more than the standard 1/- (5p) for 20 were confined to pretentious females and pansies.

Some brands included coupons, for which a zillion could be exchanged for household items which one would be unlikely to buy, not because they could not be afforded but because you would be unlikely to want them. Uniquely, Kensitas at one time offered 'Flags of the Nations' printed on artificial silk (Rayon), but most included a card with a picture on the front and a brief, relevant text in the back.

Players sold their cigarettes under the slogan 'Players Please', although they did not seem to please the grimly bearded seaman in the packet and he was not even smoking one. They certainly pleased us since they produced the best and most 'Swappable' cards and happily they must have pleased smokers since they were the most popular brand. I rather missed out on this 'Win win' situation since my father gave up smoking when I was very young and Pricey, my sole accessible uncle, rolled his own. Thus I was forced to target parents' childless friends or stand outside tobacconists, soliciting emerging g customers.

When cards of cars were around they could be run along a wall accompanied by engine noises or if they were of aeroplanes, made to perform aerobatics accompanied by zooming noises.

However since cards came in themed sets of 50, which could be stuck in little albums given away by the shops, the more serious type of young citizen concentrated on filling the album. There were Footballers, Tennis stars, Cricketers, Aeroplanes and Cars. The Cricketers series was not thought much of, even by the cricketing lobby since it was mainly Yorkshire, and Surrey players who were depicted, none from Glamorgan. Much the same for the other sports men and women. Wild Flowers were shunned as being a girls' thing, aeroplanes were OK but the star series was the car set. The problem with the sets was that the cards were not evenly distributed, 48 or 49 no problem but there were always one or two that were like hens teeth. Those of moderate rarity could be readily swapped but there were others that were so common that everyone had at least an unmarketable half doze. With the car set, had any boy been able to get his hands a spare Citroën, he could have named his own price. Parents, relatives, elder siblings and unsuspecting passers-by were badgered, probably into early graves, in pursuit of that elusive fiftieth card.

14

Cars and Capabilities

Our interest in cars did not of course include Morris Minors, Austin Sevens, Singer Juniors, or indeed the larger offering by those manufacturers or for that matter, Hillmans, Vauxhalls, Standards or Beans – we set our sights on higher things. Somehow Rolls Royces did not figure in our aspirations, but Bentleys certainly did, not the effete re-badged Rollers but the real machines, big, open, green, with an exhaust pipe a cat could crawl up. There was just one in the town, the size of a small locomotive, only locomotives just puffed, this rumbled and roared like an angry apparition. The other object of awe, a long, low, scarlet SS III was effete by comparison. I recall a glimpsed Delage and a Delahaye and a Bugatti, the latter a wreck in Lloyd's Blackpill garage, whose worth then was certainly a far cry from modern seven figure valuations. Not as redolent of the exotic as were the Continental offerings but with an air of effortless opulence that would today be called vulgarity, were the curvaceously chromed 'Big Yanks', favoured by those enjoying an unaccustomed modicum of affluence. So-called sports cars were making an appearance, the Riley Nine in various guises, Triumphs, Lea-Francis', Crossleys. Some with Dickey Seats, a few with that odd affectation the 'Boat' body, 2-seaters with the after parts finished to look like a ship's deck complete with miniature dummy ventilators.

SSs were appearing before mutating into Jaguars, and in a smaller form the MGs, the Austin 7 Sports, the Wolseley Hornets and the Singer Le Mans. Standing only a little below the Bentley was the Lagonda and for the ultimate in roartiness and naughtiness was the Aston Martin. Then there were the Daimlers favoured by royalty, followed by Lanchesters, and Armstrong Sidderlys, plus standing out on its own the Rover, ownership of which announced that the owner had made it into Rotary and Golf club territory.' The sedate Humber and the Wolseley saloons (Glorified Morris Old Boy!) were too sobersides to be appealing as in all honesty was the 20 hp (Yes Twenty!) horsepower, imagine it!) Austin that chauffer driven was a 'school run' vehicle for two brothers. A similarly large, and similarly chauffeur-driven vehicle, which collected another boy, had an aura of the exotic being an aged Isotta Francini.

We were beginning to see more 'Big Yanks', such as Buicks and Chryslers (The Chrysler Airlow, streamliner for instance), which enabled a serious statement of self-importance could be made with a minimum of expenditure. There was even one example of a big black and chrome Brough Superior a not entirely successful attempt by George Brough to make a car that would be as pre-eminent as were his motorcycles.

There were still examples of cars from an earlier age, Renaults with 'Coal-scuttle' bonnets and spindly, upright offerings with a spare wheel on each side and a 2-gallon spare petrol tin clamped to the running board. There was a doctor with an 'Electric Carriage', like an enormous invalid carriage that crept at a walking pace conned by the worthy medico grasping a tiller.

My ambitions were more modest; my vehicle of choice for pulling birds on say the Promenade des Anglais at Nice or perhaps Sunset Boulevard would have been a Morgan three-wheeler. Not of course the effete 'runabouts' with four seats and an engine lurking behind a heart-shaped cut out, but the real McCoy – the Aero. I visualised big Vee-twin J.A.P. engine proudly displaying its dancing push-rods, propelling me capped and goggled, my elbow gripping the cutaway side, my backside an inch from the ground, the growl of the chrome exhaust pipes on either side, causing every head to turn. In fact it would be a very adventurous young lady who would chance chignon or her chastity in one of these. It may be of course that I realised that it would be adventurous young ladies that I would be seeking!

Actually of course, for most of the few people who could afford cars it was those head to head rivals Austin with their Seven and Morris with their Minor. Vauxhall with its smallest offering being the faintly flashy 'Fourteen' was out of the mass market, likewise Ford who had replaced the Model T with the less than popular Model A and later, the spectacular V-8, good value but even with the smaller 22 h. p. engine, too big for the Brash market. However they re-entered the big-time with the 1934 £100 Ford 8.

This put the solid but unexciting Hillman Minx out of contention for third place behind Austin and Morris. Their Aero Minx was a gallant attempt to spice up the Minx, but it was only when transmogrified into the

Sunbeam-Talbot did it achieve a fashionably rakish image. M of

It is not easy at this distance to realise how fierce was the Austin/Morris rivalry. At a time when 10/- (50p) could swing a sale, pricing was predatory. Custom dictated that prices were declared for the year at each Autumn Motor Show so to get it wrong was serious. Each of the two contenders trying to second-guess the opposition's prices. There were tales that each had departments devoted to pricing espionage. Pricing apart each tried to carve out a market niche. Austin nurtured a perception of acumen into buying their products with the slogan *You buy a car but you invest in an Austin.* Morris countered by developing a reputation for innovation and were first with such things as hydraulic brakes and unitary construction although oddly they clung to the central accelerator long after the present right-hand position had become near universal.

My childhood was divided into two parts, before 10 and after 10, the cusp of this watershed being The Car. Car ownership was gradually becoming a respectable middle-class aspiration, overcoming obstacles that were not entirely financial. Car ownership had begun amongst the 'Carriage Folk' the upper strata that could afford the not inconsiderable cost of feeding and accommodating both a horse and driver. Racy young bucks might buy a car and drive it themselves but respectable people employed a driver. Driving and maintaining a motor vehicle was considered so specialised that apparently in the early days only a Frenchman could master both skills

– hence the French name still applied to a private car driver.

By my time of course, when most business and professional men had cars, which they not only drove themselves but even allowed their wives to drive. Doctors were an exception, although cars had emerged from the roadside repair stage, punctures were still frequent so the dirtying of hands was not considered good medical practice, hence most employed drivers.

My early personal experience of motoring was very constrained. Wealthy friends occasionally allowed me to drive their pedal cars, and in the kindergarten there was a rota of fathers to drive us weekly to the YMCA gym.

I recall being in the back of a 'tourer' on a sightseeing trip. It was raining hard. The roof leaked and the celluloid side screens were misted up so there were no sights to see. More vividly remembered is my only ride in a dickey seat. (This was an arrangement whereby a two seater would have a boot with a bottom-hinged lid that opened up to reveal a seat, the lid being padded to form the back). A family friend of Professor and Mrs Hughes was Captain Crawsay (Of the Ironmaster dynasty). One Summer's day the good Captain proposed a motorcar ride to Mrs Hughes. Such an excursion could not take place unchaperoned so her son Geraint and I were pressed into service. Captain Crawshay's car was a modest two-seater so Geraint and I were relegated to the dickey along with a supply of rock cakes, which we were enjoined on no account to eat. However Geraint used them as missiles to throw at cyclists and pedestrians so by the time we stopped at our destination Tor Bay, there were none left. The trouble was that Geraint blamed me protesting that he had tried to stop me!

Motoring took a more personal dimension when my father decided to 'Go in for' a car. The showrooms were toured, Armstrong Sidderlys and Lanchesters were of course out of the question as were Rovers. Regrettably a Riley or an MG could not be considered. Since Ford were yet to launch their '£100 Eight' the choice came down to an Austin or a Morris. Both firms offered a range of cars from the Austin Seven and the Morris Minor (Later the '8') through 10, 12, 14 horsepower up to the grand 'Twenty-fives' most being offered as saloons, cabriolets and 2 and 4-seater tourers.

I fancied the perky open 2-seater Austin Seven, but this was displaced in my ambitions in 1935 by the Morris Eight. The saloons were unexceptional, but the open 2-seater was something else – low, rakish and with a cutaway door that just begged for an elbow to be hooked over it – a real 'poor man's MG'.

Obviously in my father's case canvas and side screens were out, a saloon it had to be. There really was 'no contest' with Austin marketing department's carefully constructed air of financial prudence, he could buy no other. Scorning the 'Seven' at around £120, father sprang the £172.10.0 for the 'Ten, Saloon De-luxe'. There was of course a 'Standard' version without indicators, bumpers and such, at around £160, but you would have been hard pressed to obtain one –it would have to be specially made! Even so it turned out to be a special order. It had to be black (In case it was used for funerals), my mother insisted on green upholstery, but my father wanted a brown line along each side, which only came with brown upholstery, but Messrs Austin obliged at no extra charge, Costs had been carefully studied and they did mount up. £10 Tax, nearly as much for insurance and each and every galloon of petrol, at least a 1/- (5p). On top of this there was maintenance, with a dozen or more nipples (A snigger word if ever there was one!) to be greased every 500 miles. So with depreciation (Whatever that was) motoring could cost £1 per week, a quarter of a respectable wage packet.

The world is occupied by people who are natural drivers, by people who with application become adequate drivers and those who no matter how assiduously they apply themselves, never quite grasp the basic skills of the road. My father was in the latter category.

Fortunately he had as his mechanical mentor Frank Reed, his foreman driver, a quiet and patient man who had been a horse handler and taught himself to drive, maintain and even make parts for the Firm's vehicles. Even so father was fortunate to just scrape in ahead of the introduction of Driving Tests.

He treated the pedals like switches, i.e. either on or off, so that departures and stops were liable to be abrupt, the latter often accompanied by a rear-end shunt. The trauma of upward gear changes could be reduced by starting in second, or with the assistance of a favourable gradient third or even fourth. Changing down was a last desperate gamblers throw when even the use of choke and zigzagging to ease the gradient failed. Hill starts he best accomplished by using the kerb as a chock. Reverse parking or indeed reversing of any kind, he dismissed as 'Showing off'. Although basically a law-abiding man and was himself Chairman of Magistrates, he regarded speed limits as purely advisory and a red traffic light as a warning to exert caution at busy crossings Nevertheless, although he investigated hedges occasionally, he drove that Austin 10 for 16 years and its Austin A40 successor for 10, he never had a serious accident.

Oddly, motorcycles did not seem to figure on my wish lists, although I recall pressing my nose against the window of a shop in Cradock Street, drooling over Indian motorcycles, vast fire engine red four-cylinder monsters. And I also recall the reverse-capped, one-eyed gent who cruised the town on an FN motorcycle and sidecar with four slender cylinders sticking up from the engine like factory chimneys.

Looming larger in our thoughts were trains, as was inevitable in a town criss-crossed by passenger, goods and docks railways and its head-count of main line termini probably only exceeded by London. Indeed a sizeable minority travelled to school by train. The engine driver ambition was already passé and one sensed a hint of obsolescence even then. However train spotting was popular, not the modern collecting of numbers, but a far more exciting version. Almost all the many stations within the town's boundaries had a passenger over-bridge, usually with open-lattice sides. With a great deal of luck a patient wait after dark, would be rewarded by a train stopping with the chimney of the locomotive in close juxtaposition with the bridge. The intention (never as far as I am aware achieved) being to pee down the chimney with the aim of putting out the fire.

Such pleasures were confined to the dark winter evenings, another equally seasonal interest was 'Guy Fawkes' Not that my set was concerned with dragging a Guy around begging for pennies, or the 'Fireworks Parties' where one was supposed to gape at Catherine Wheels or Roman Candles, and certainly not childish sparklers. Rockets were all right but were much more interesting if discharged horizontally. Girl scaring with Jackie Jumpers was all right too, but the main things were Bangers!!

In those days Bangers were not the pathetic Health & Safety controlled apologies for bangers sold today. Then even a halfpenny banger made a proper bang and when one moved into 1d, or ever 2d territory, you had a real window-rattler. In the days prior to November 5th much ingenuity was employed in maximising the potential of Black Powder. A lightweight vessel such as an old milk saucepan or enamelled chamber pot could be made to soar to spectacular heights if inverted over a sizzling banger. The usual target being telephone wires. Building sites invariably had a pit filled with semi-liquid lime and a banger stuck in made an impressive crater and delivered a blizzard of lime.

For those of us sufficiently attentive in the Physics class to have acquired a smattering of Thermo-dynamics realised that containment was the secret of real success. A particularly satisfying exercise was to obtain one of the 10-inch cube biscuit tins then used for the containment and display of biscuits in shops (no easy task since there was a 1/- (5p) deposit on them!)

One would take the largest banger one could afford and drop it into a biscuit tin, when it started to sizzle banged the lid on, put a brick on the lid to prevent it being harmlessly blown off, and retire very quickly indeed. The result was total destruction of the tin and an explosion of near Richter-scale magnitude.

Some boys tried to make gunpowder, but this (fortunately!) only resulted in a brief but fierce flash. One boy, who was particularly bright at Chem, was convinced he could make nitro-glycerine, fortunately he was mistaken.

Had we realised it, the time was close when we would become familiar with much bigger bangs.

15

Aims and Ambitions

'What are you going to do when you grow up?' was a constant mantra. Being a cowboy had its attractions, as did prospecting for gold. The building of railways in South America, or administering the outposts of Empire (wherever that meant) was parentally peddled, but like anything considered suitable involved 'Studying hard' which made it unattractive. The Foreign Legion was briefly in the frame, but the overall inclination was towards engineering until I discovered it did not necessarily have anything to do with engines but boring stuff like bridges and things. So what? Anyone could build a bridge, my friend Geoffrey and I regularly made bridges across the stream at the back of his house – even dammed it some times creating reservoirs. We even had thoughts of collecting discarded bricks from nearby building sites with the aim of building a bridge to the moon, a project abandoned at teatime when despite a hard afternoon's graft we had only collected eleven bricks.

There was a fleeting thought of being a doctor but I fear rather from the opportunities which it offered to own a posh car and to see ladies naked, than high ideals of effecting cures. But staying roughly in the curative sector being a garage mechanic had attractions – able to mend broken cars and with the bonus of an opportunity to nonchalantly drive all sorts of cars with one's elbow resting on the windowsill. But such things involved getting one's hands dirty, which apparently was big no-no.

Seeing some of the self-employed agents who called on my father turned my thoughts towards another direction – they had cars. Hillmans the size of a bus, Vee-8 Fords, Rovers even, or in one case a Bentley, not one of the pansy Rolls-Bentleys but the long, leather-strapped bonneted, mile-a-minute McCoy. These of course were men at the top of their profession, real 'Gentlemen of the Road', but even quite modest 'reps' were being provided with cars. Admittedly only small Morris' or Austins, or later on Ford 8s, were pretty basic stuff really, but a car nevertheless and one was beginning to realise that such vehicles were not to be sneered at since they had, as we would later realise, a vital accoutrement lacking in MGs and the like, a back seat. Unfortunately a 'firm's' car, having been registered at the firm's headquarters, the letters on the number plate would be unfamiliar. Sapient young ladies would inspect a number plate before accepting a lift home. They would realise that almost any combination of letters other than the familiar WN spelt REP, indicating that it was safer to walk.

The attritions of a career in peripatetic peddling were dramatically enhanced by the announcement of the 1939 Morris 8. Until then the style, comfort and appointments of the smallest cars were clearly intended to make one chose a larger and more expensive vehicle, the new Morris 8 changed that, it seemed a veritable miniature limousine.

Endeavours to engage my father in meaningful discussion regarding a career usually resulted in a mumbled, 'You need a haircut'. Actually my distaste of haircuts was well founded, the barber to which I was taken had the habit of pulling away the scissors before finishing each cut, so that at the end of snip, hairs were torn out by the roots. One of my strongest incentives to join the forces was to distance myself from this awful man. The first real opportunity to have a civilian haircut was at Wolverhampton where I was immediately attacked in the same manner – by the same man!

Not all my father's advice was negative; he did succeed in inculcating a life-long sense of financial prudence. Good advice in his day but in modern conditions where prudence is penalised and profligacy encouraged, such advice has proved of limited value. This advice was largely subliminal, the only direct advice I ever recall was 'Never to have anything to do with the Masons'. Whether this was good or bad advice I have yet to discover.

Seriously drawn towards the monumental, I had a brief affair with architecture although parental injunction had by then veered towards teaching or the Civil Service (Whatever that was). There were stern warnings that a boy must know what he wanted to do by the time he reached 15. I knew what I wanted to do but as I have said I did not realise that there could be money in it, anyway pimpled and overweight, I would scarcely meet the Job Description, thus as I approached that age I became increasingly anxious. A friend had taken a job as a Telegram Boy raced about on a motorcycle – indeed a RED motorcycle – that was even better than being a rep and having a car. The snag was that at 18 they took the bike away and made you a postman but since this involved getting up early and walking was ruled out.

Some years before I had seen the Great Cyclino (Aka Harry Holmes, stage door-keeper of the local Empire music hall), dressed up as a cat, juggling three batons while seated on an absolutely stationary bicycle. My father introduced me to him and having caught his batons and tucked them under his arm, had offered me a paw to shake, all without putting a foot to the ground. Much as I wished to emulate him, hours spent repeatedly falling off my bicycle (without even attempting to juggle) had long convinced me that I was not cyclo-feline material.

However, by a process of gradual osmosis rather than by Damascene revelation – I knew what I wanted to do.

I would like to think the seed was sown when my father first introduced me to Sir Arthur Whiten Brown. Much to the embarrassment of this over-modest man, it had been explained to me that he had been the first man to fly an aeroplane non-stop across the Atlantic Ocean. It did occur to me that if one were going to successfully fly the Atlantic Ocean it would have to be non-stop. But I could not connect this very ordinary looking man with a great hero of the skies. (This was before I discovered that unlike Batman or Superman, real-life heroes look like ordinary people). Anyway pilots heroic or otherwise, wore goggles, not over their eyes like motorcyclists but on their foreheads like sacred phylacteries. Pilots wore leather helmets, not bowler hats; their coats were leather not cloth, so its impact on me at the time was minimal.

When my classmates rushed to the schoolroom window at the sound of a distant, asthmatic motorbike, hoping usually in vain, of glimpsing a contraption stagger uncertainly across the sky, I hung back in a most blasé manner since I had not just seen, but almost touched, an aeroplane! It had been on the sands at low tide, quite near Brynmill, where there was, in those days a stream of dammable and splash-aboutable-in, potential. What is more, it was not just any old aeroplane; it was a War Plane! It had been, as later cigarette card research would reveal, an Avro 504K, an ex World War (Pre-World War in fact!) machine, one of thousands that could be bought for little more than the price of a push bike AND it was giving rides. There was no question of doing so myself since it would cost the massive sum of 5/- (25) and the parental view was that there were cheaper ways of committing suicide. I recall closely examining the external control wires of the machine and noting that the elevators were down and that the joystick was forward so was able to work out how the latter had to be pushed or pulled to go down or up. (In effect my first flying lesson).

I suppose the real seeds of aeronautical ambition were sown on a bright and sunny Whit Monday in 1933 by courtesy of British Hospitals Air Pageants, one of several 'Air Circus' that in the mid to late 1930s would take a swarm of aeroplanes around the country doing displays and giving five shilling (25p) rides.

It all took place from a field some miles out of town

at Parc LeBreos and considering that at that time flying was regarded much as bungee jumping is today, it was surprisingly well attended. In fact the buses did record business although the conductors were reluctant to issue return tickets to anyone expressing an intention of actually going up. Such misgivings were well founded, the field was rough and steeply sloping, partly surrounded by trees and quite unsuitable for aviational use, had I known then what I know now I would not have entertained any idea of going up. As it was I could only try to contain my excitement at being almost within touching distance of aeroplanes, Avro 504s. Tiger Moths and others including a Fox Moth, which was a somewhat bloated Tiger Moth with the front cockpit missing, but submerged in the fuselage was a tiny 4-seat cabin like a miniature railway compartment.

I succeeded not only in persuading my father to fund a flight, but all that a 30 minute 'Air Cruse' at 20/- (children half price) was far better value than a 5 minute 5/- job with no juvenile discount. I have to be honest and say that the flight itself was all something of a disappointment, partly because my father insisted on accompanying me, thus the more exciting Avros and Moths were out of the question, he demanded that we fly in the largest and newest and so presumably the safest machine available.

My father was slightly uneasy at being told that such a machine was of De Havilland manufacture, the name having Gallic, and therefore untrustworthy, connotations. However on being assured that a machine of this make had recently conveyed Miss Amy Johnson safely to Australia, that this particular type was incapable of performing stunts and had the reassuringly Welsh name of Dragon, he relented.

It was a DH 84, the very latest in twin-engined biplanes and with as many as 8 seats was entitled to call itself an Air Liner. But the interior was a double disappointment not only did it resemble a small and exiguously equipped tramcar on a stiff gradient but the pilot was goggle-less, had no leather helmet or flying suit, not even a cap back-to-front – just a blazer and a straw hat! The Air Cruise was a formation flight the Dragon leading a gaggle of five assorted types. There was no sense of speed and none of height, the view resembling an elaborately detailed model layout, the only sense of movement being the gentle rise and falling of the formating machines.

Back on the ground there were other attractions; various vertiginous aerobatics and the near 200 mph fly-past by the glinting polished aluminium of the latest manifestation of Britain's aerial might –the Hawker Fury. The highlight was the celebrated Welsh pilot, Idwal Jones' speciality of picking a 'handkerchief' (Actually more a tea towel) with the wingtip of his Tiger Moth.

There were subsequent 'Air Circus' opportunities to fly, fortunately at the flatter and larger Vennway field. An Airspeed Ferry, a sort of three-engined miniature simulacrum of the mighty Hercules' of Imperial Airways, the little twin-engined General Monospar, and the inevitable Avro 504 two-seaters, re-engined and modified to carry three passengers, but retaining its 'Trade mark'; skid between the wheels to prevent nose-overs, thus generating a useful 15/- (75p) of revenue, the fuel cost of 2 or 3 hours flying in what was little more than a wide circuit.

Any aviational aspirations had remained dormant under a rock-fall of parental disapproval. Of course they may have had a point, the aeroplane has not proved to be the most beneficial of inventions, it has brought death and disaster, it has polluted the atmosphere with noxious fumes and Mediterranean beaches with noxious persons, but in the 1930s it was still redolent both of chivalry and of reaching places such as Baghdad and Allahabad (wherever they were) faster than they had ever been reached before. It was a mystery as to why reaching such places in record time, or indeed reaching them at all, was such a big deal, but apparently it was something to do with the Empire and Showing the Flag whatever that meant.

Approaching this decade an half decision time, the seeds germinated and my memory of that first Air Circus came back, not of the machines nor even the unexpected pheromonic smells, but the Hon. Mrs Victor Bruce the then celebrated aviatrix, immaculately dressed in a white flying suit and looking like a bifurcated Seraphim. It came to me that if I were to soar to the skies and ride the wind I would be doing it with the birds in both meanings of the word. The second meaning did not (yet!) entirely arise through concupiscence but, I regret to admit, from chauvinistic thoughts that if girls could fly, so might even I.

It was at this point that the parents started to resort

to guile; rather than showing shock and horror, they did agree that it all might be possible, provided I did much better in school, kept my bedroom tidy and ate up my cabbage (and got my hair cut!). It took me a long time to suss this con trick. In my realistic moments I was weighed down by the realisation that I would never be able to afford any of the pleasures that aviation seemed to offer.

Then the adverts started to appear on the hoardings urging everyone to join the RAF – they showed the RAF man, clearly an officer, clean-cut, staring into the wide blue yonder, wings on his chest, and aeroplane in the background and a WAAF at his side. I thought problem solved – the parents had always talked about 'Getting in with a big firm', surely firms did not come much bigger than the Air Force and whereas even the biggest firm would only give you a car, the RAF would give you an aeroplane. In addition, the juxtaposition of the man and the woman inferred that complimentary crumpet was part of the deal. This was another con trick, the chances of becoming a pilot let alone an officer pilot were negligible and as for the WAAFs – forget it. Had the Trades Description Act been in force in those days, I am sure that the Air Marshals would have found themselves in serious bother.

What they also did not tell you was that if you bucked the odds and found yourself in command of one of His Gracious Majesty's flying machines it would be liable to be a derivative of one that had been all the rage in 1917. Admittedly RAF machines had flown over Everest and the RAF was keeping peace in Iraq with wartime-armoured cars, but little else.

We were heartened to hear of the new Wellesley bomber's epic 7000-mile flight, and of the Bristol Blenheim, so fast that even the Hawker Super Fury could not catch it (The new Germans fighters could!) We were even enjoined to praise the Fairey Battle that could be outrun and outgunned by more or less anything.

However things were changing, I remember leaning my bicycle against the fence of RAF Marham and standing on the crossbar to snatch a furtive glimpse of the brooding bulk of the mighty but super-secret Wellington. Soon to be emblazoned across the front pages the fact that a Hurricane had flown from Edinburgh to London at a much-trumpeted 409 mph. The publicity failed to mention the gale-force tailwind!

The fires of enthusiasm were further stoked by rumours of another, much faster machine, which was so secret that it ws rumoured that it was only test-flown at night.

Meanwhile the 'Royal Advertising Farce' relentlessly maintained its offers of lots of lovely lolly to do a job that most boys would do for nothing. Cleary it was a case of 'Many are called nut few are chosen' thus the prospects of the likes of any of us griping the control column of one of these wonder machines seemed very remote.

Then one sunny Sunday morning the Prime Minister made a broadcast at the end of which the air raid sirens (Mistakenly as it turned out) sounded their warning.

This was seen by adults as a matter for fear and sadness – regrettably, some of us saw it as an opportunity.

16

War

Our concept of war had been forged in the YMCA cinema on Saturday mornings where the goodies in the white hats put the black-hatted baddies to flight on a weekly basis and if the worst came to the worst, the Seventh2 Cavalry would arrive in the nick of time. In any case we knew that after the end of the film the casualties would get up and enjoy a nice cup of tea with their attackers. Alternatively, war could be the Boys Own Paper vision of a white man armed with nothing more than a cricket bat, 'teaching a lesson' to fuzzy-wuzzies, dagoes and dirty foreigners of every sort. If our attention was directed to real conflict we saw it as revolver-brandishing British officers charging unscathed through a hail of bullets, or Biggles in his aeroplane shooting down Red Barons on a daily basis.

Those of us who had been on the Easter 1939 School Trip saw things rather differently. It was the first trip I had been on since in previous years I had been under the 14 age minimum. These trips were intended to improve our grasp of foreign lingos and were usually to France or Germany, this one was to Belgium so the first part at least was a failure being Flemish Ostend based, where even then, any attempt to speak French was to invite a thumping. Not that that worried us, we were 'Only there for the beer' (and the cheap champagne and fags) all of which could be purchased by sign language. We did have problems seeking a light for the ciggies, not realising that 'Have you fire?' was the term, no wonder people kept on giving us 60 Watt bulbs.

We were lead by our dear headmaster, but fair play, the other masters suspended their normal Pinky-baiting to save him from making too much of a mess of things and too much a fool of himself. We, I am sorry to say were not so generous and our dodging about so that his head count was always wrong reduced him to trembling incoherence. Apart from the inevitable inter-compartment fights on the train our behaviour was by and large impeccable. There was of course the misreading of the drinks price list at the Casino, but the Gendarmerie were most understanding and a few francs from the head master's emergency float soon settled matters.

At Brussels the matter of imitating the *Manikin Pis* from the hotel balcony was regrettable, but most of the people in the street below had umbrellas to put up so no harm was done. It is to our credit that we were always ready to assist any master who, late at night, was seen to have ambulation issues.

Heavily overlaying the frivolity was a darker side, everywhere were men in uniform, not squaddies out on a jolly but seriously intent men with rifles slung across their backs, out in country the 'Dragon's Teeth' of tank traps, avenues with the trees belted with explosive ready to be dropped in an invader's path. Everywhere there were the red posters and graffiti of the openly pro-German Rexists, glowering at the even redder posters of the Communists. The whole country seemed a pressure-cooker poised to explode. Mr. Chamberlain might believe that a 'Screp of paypah' would bring 'Peace in ewer tim', but we had seen for ourselves that we were on a slippery slope.

That the slope would not lead to a game of cowboys and Indians, but Armageddon II, was dramatically proclaimed by the Menin Gate, covered graffiti-like with countless thousands of names of men who otherwise have not a particle of dust to mark their brief life on earth. Even more the row upon row of white grave-stones juxtaposed with guardsmen's precision, marching to the far horizons. And the battlefields', zig-zags of trenches their scars healed green, bestrewn with shell fragments and cartridge cases that having done their deadly work become tourist souvenirs.

Back home spy scares abounded Herr Keller (Hell Killer) the German master was 'Definitely' known' to possess powerful binoculars and even the inoffensive little French student teacher was seen with a rucksack that 'Obviously' contained a camera. The Graf Zeppelin was seen over Swansea Bay allegedly with telescopic lenses trained on the docks. A friend of somebody's brother 'Definitely' saw a man with a German accent buying up maps in W H Smith. A man in a black leather overcoat was seen in Swansea Market clicking his heels when asking for 'Zee Kockles.'

On the other hand there were the stories that the German tanks seen on newsreels were made of cardboard and the fly-pasts of hordes of German aircraft were the same few going round and round like a stage army. In the meantime while not actively 'Seeking a bubble reputation even in the cannon's mouth' and not even really all that anxious to 'Do one's bit', we did not wish to be mere classroom onlookers, so could only hope that matters would be postponed until we were old enough to take part.

It would have to be the RAF, not just from a built-in Biggles complex, but a preference for going to war sitting down and wishing to sleep in a reasonably safe bed, ruled out both the Army and the Navy.

Following that Sunday morning broadcast, there was almost a sense of anticlimax that the sky was not black with German aircraft, raining high explosive and mustard gas. So began the 'Phoney War'.

Everyone carried a gas mask in a small but awkward cardboard box and was enjoined by posters to do this or that and suchlike. Soon almost everything was rationed or in 'Short supply'. Or 'Don't make me laugh, there's a war on' seemed to be the universal catchphrases when trying to make the simplest purchase. There was a strict blackout, the showing of any light was prohibited and anyone with a seaward facing home who even briefly showed a glimpse of light was accused of signalling to German submarines. Speaking of which everyone knew someone who had a friend in west Wales who recounted tales of German submarine crews coming ashore to have a beer in seaside pubs or of nautically-attired persons calling at post offices to enquire in a strange accent, the cost of sending a post card to Germany. A rather inoffensive university lecturer who had been appointed an Official War Photographer was lucky to escape a lynching when seen taking snaps with a German camera.

The keeper of one shop with a slightly Germanic name on its facia, was at pains to point out that he was Lithuanian, which was liable to earn rejoinders of the 'We don't care what chapel you go to, wuss', variety. This feeling took an ugly turn when Italy declared war and all the Italian Cafés were trashed, a discreditable episode which the town took a generation to live down.

What one's father did in the 'Last War' became a matter of playground boast. I suffered the handicap of having a father whose military experience was gained in the Glamorgan Volunteers (The precursors of the Territorial), standing guard on the coast lest the dastardly Boers invaded. I could only gape at accounts by other fathers of single-handed charges at massed enemy ranks, of medals refused and turning down commissions as they wished to stay with their comrades. I had yet to learn that bravery and bragging do not co-habit.

There was obviously a need to restrict what was said in the papers and on the wireless, but when there is no news people invent their own. Added to which everyone liked to be thought of as being 'In the know.' The result was that everyone had the most outlandish tales that were supposed to be 'Hush-hush', but had been told them 'On the Q T'.

All this was stoked by the mock upper class drawl of Lord Haw Haw, the 'Jarminy Cawling' propagandist who everyone listened to but few took seriously. Plus there were the 'Armchair experts' who knew everything 'For a fact', having a knowledge of military tactics far beyond the ken of our Generals. There was, perhaps fortunately, an atmosphere of ridiculous optimism. Even when Germany overran Denmark and Norway in days, even the Prime Minister hailed it as a strategic mistake. Saying that, 'Hitler has missed the bus'. Special praise went to the RAF for their nightly 'Pounding of Germany' – with leaflets! With apparently orders not to throw out whole bundles in case they hurt anyone! The invasion of the Low Countries and France came and went as did the 'Strategic Withdrawal' at Dunkirk.

People claimed to have seen air battles over Swansea Bay, but these were old Whitley bombers from Stormy Down carrying trainee air-gunners shooting at drogues drawn by Hawker Henleys. Actually our first 'Taste of War' came just after the fall of France when one morning a French aircraft flew over Swansea docks, bombing and machine-gunning with, unfortunately some loss of life. It has never been established if the aeroplane was flown by Germans hoping, correctly, that bearing French markings would not be attacked, or whether it was flown by anti-British Frenchmen. Confined to a frosted-glass windowed classroom we heard the raid but to our annoyance could not see it.

The high point of the summer of 1940 and a theoretical contribution to the War Effort was the school forestry camp high in hills on the headwaters of the river Towy. Some masters accompanied us but the head master's involvement was minimal, so it was only minimally shambolic. We reached there by a complicated combination of bus and train to sleep in various assorted tents close to the riverbank. We were given three meals (of a sort) per day prepared by an ancient character alleged to have been a ship's cook (Who called the cook a bastard? Who called the bastard a cook?) In addition to which we received actual real wages, The rate was 6d (2½p) per hour which to a lad receiving half a crown (12½p) per week pocket money was new-found wealth.

Since the weather was hot, it was an immediate attraction having a convenient pool at the foot of a small waterfall. The fact that we had not packed 'Bathers' did not discourage us from a good splash in the refreshing waters. It was rumoured that one of the masters' wives had more than once 'accidentally' passed our makeshift Lido. However when one of the bigger boys (In more than one sense) stood on an overhanging rock and did a *Manikin Pis* act onto the bathers, she fled the scene.

As someone said, forestry work involved 'Cutting trees down and then cutting them up'. We learned the argot, thick trees were 'Timber' thin trees were 'Poles' and lines of felling running up the hillside were called 'Ranches'. We were sensibly kept well away from the felling but received the pollarded timber and pole at the foot of the ranch. Being immature Pine there was little timber but plenty of poles that had to be sawn into pit-props or if too short for this, the ends had to be pointed like sharpening a pencil to form pickets for securing the barbed wire entanglements which were appearing everywhere as Invasion loomed. We had quotas to meet and periodically our output would be counted by a visiting foreman, who blue-chalked the end of each pit prop or picket counted. It was found less of an effort to rub out the chalk mark than to chop and saw fresh output.

Now with lads unused to serious wood work being let loose with machetes and big, two-handed saws, some attempts to sever fingers was inevitable, when the accidental amputation of hands seemed a possibility, first-aid provisions were mad and each ranch had its own dedicated first-aider. Sitting around with a bag of bandages seemed preferable to actually working, so on the strength of having attended a lecture on the subject, I volunteered as a first aider.

Back home we could only await attainment of the magical 'Military age', anyone, no matter how slow of wit or short of sight, nurtured intentions to be a pilot' especially as apart from flying it would provide a uniform that was reputedly irresistible to women. There were those who counselled caution, pointing out that proverbially 'Nice girls love a sailor.' An enjoiner countered by the suggestion that it was not the nice girls one wished to attract. One lad was jeered at for showing an interest in joining the Army, but he got the last laugh by ending up a Major General.

Certainly after the Battle of Britain, the blue uniform of even the scruffiest Aircraftman Second Class exuded aphrodisiac redolence. It was said that even the similarly hued garb of RAC patrolmen caused its wearers to cower in gentlemen's lavatories to escape importunate females.

Anyway the war did transform aviational aspirations from a whim to be grown out of, into a patriotic duty. Furthermore joining the RAF guaranteed that one did one's patriotic duty and still avoid the discomforts and inconveniences associated with the other Services. Of course the possibility of finding oneself in the RAF in a non-flying capacity was too terrible to dwell upon.

There were I am pleased to say, moral scruples about killing people, and the 'What if a great big Nazi Storm Trooper was going to rape your sister' cut little ice with me since I had no sister and the sisters of my friends were in the main, such little prigs, one would be reluctant to get involved, particularly if the chap was all that big. However we were assured that one would only be called upon to kill Germans, which was apparently OK.

Our impatience to be old enough to join up was in no way diminished by lurid newspaper accounts of scandalous 'goings on' between service men and women. Such stories may well have been official inventions to boost recruiting and I am sure that many male recruits were disappointed to find that service women were treated as family members, and anyway were assiduously corralled behind barbed wire, sentinelled by female military police of generous build and Sapphic inclinations.

Even the more serious side of wartime life was a source of diversion; the air raids gave the opportunity to collect shrapnel and unexploded incendiary bombs. Fortunately few if any of my contemporaries suffered harm or serious domestic damage, and the destruction of the school by enemy action could not be viewed as totally tragic, in fact working a two-shift system in neighbouring premises afforded a degree of excitement. Further excitement was derived from acting as messengers for the ARP (Air Raid Precautions) street wardens, which gained one a steel helmet and even an armband. A friend and I were on one occasion pressed into service by a Bomb Disposal team. This particular unexploded bomb had been dug out of a basement area and defused, but due to the number of demands being made upon the squad, they had to leave just one soldier to drag it up the steps to pavement level to await collection. The raising of some 100Kg of smooth, muddy and incompliant steel, proved too much for the man' who called upon two gawking schoolboys (us!) to assist. We did get the bomb almost all the way up, but at the top step it escaped our grasp to descend crashing onto each step in an accelerating crescendo of resounding thuds. There was no explosion but by the time it had come to rest we were in the next street.

Adults tut-tutted and deplored the wartime loosening of morals, and doubtless there were women ready to 'Lay themselves down for their country', but search as we might we encountered nothing of this. There was one example of the slightly distorted mores of the time, when the parents of a boy from the form next above travelled home on the overnight train a day early, to find that their son and heir had taken advantage of the neighbours also being away to entertain their daughter in his parents' bed. His mother's distress arose not from the customary causes but from having at a time of stringent food rationing, to provide the girl with breakfast.

Initially at least, one impact of the war was to widen the scope of schoolboy humour, 'The Italians have taken Cascara and are now rushing to the Po', 'What do you think of the Japanese position? – Never tried it'. 'My sister went out with a Pole and came back with a Czech'. This vein was enriched by the arrival of the Americans, with such gems as 'Utility knickers? One Yank and they're down'.

The Americans had something of a bad press (Overpaid, Oversexed, Over here). Partly due to the exchange rate, they were affluent by our servicemen's standards which combined with an innate generosity and bewilderment engendered by florins and half crowns, caused them to be accused of 'Throwing their money about.' Actually their financial naivety was liable to be shamelessly exploited by barmen, taxi drivers and the like, with exchanges such as

'That'll be a tanner, mate'
'What is a tanner?'
'Half a crown.'
'How much is half a crown?'
'Five shillings.'

The Americans delighted in giving gum and 'candy' to children and cigarettes to their elders, the basic unit of the cigarettes not being a packet, but a carton of 200, albeit in flimsy paper packets of 20, bearing pictures of a camel, an animal whose droppings were alleged to be the content's raw material. Having seemingly limitless supplies of the then legendary Nylons, who can blame them if, far distant from the strict moral codes of home, they accepted gestures of gratitude from young lady recipients. By and large, young men who a few months before had never been outside the Bronx or beyond the city limits of Hicksville, coped well with what must have been a most alien environment, where people talked a funny kind of English and drove on the wrong side of the road. In the meantime we could only gape at these men with the funny walk and gaiters, and the officers whose tunics did not match their trousers, giving the impression that they had dressed in the dark. Their language was puzzling –if they wanted water they asked for a faucet, their rather fine boots they called shoes, our shoes they called slippers.

It was difficult to realise that when they talked of women sitting on their fannies, that they were, but merely reflecting their slang for the *Glutenus Maximus*. Regrettably many a GI must have suffered a slapped face for inviting a young woman to shag. (The shag being a dance transatlantically popular at the time).

To our puzzlement they all seemed to wear two medals. One seemingly showed that they had joined the army, which seemed *de trop* since their uniform was a dead give-away that they had done so. The other was for being in a war zone, which we interpreted as being somewhere like the Western Desert. It was difficult to get one's head around the fact that they classed Sketty as a war zone, where the only fighting was the occasional Saturday night punch-up outside the Vivian Arms.

The epithet 'Over-sexed', was not entirely unjustified

– young, fit and far removed from hometown restraints, paid much more than our own servicemen and with so many of our young men absent, they were well placed to fill a 'Gap in the market'. Added to which they had an inherent courtesy and generosity and wore uniforms of better cut and cloth that gave them a competitive edge. They had apparently unlimited cigarettes and nylon stockings (the first scarce the second unobtainable) so were able to repay 'favours'. Over inquisitive younger siblings could be bought off with gum and 'candy'.

Later on as the numbers mounted, coloured troops were encamped at Jersey Marine, and apparently bathed naked in the sea. This was said to be a spectacle much sought after by the boys of Port Tennant. It was also said that there were plenty of girls who would have liked to have witnessed the show but were kept away by their boyfriends, reputedly not so much from a sense of decency as a fear of the girls getting big ideas.

We (and hopefully few of them) realised how many of these charmingly naïve boys would die on Normandy beaches and Picardy fields.

17

The Escape

The spring of 1941 offered the first glimmer of escape from a bystander role – the ATC (Air Training Corps).

Hitherto apart from the Scouts and the Church Lads Brigade there had been scant opportunity for a boy to wear uniform. There were Army Cadets but these were mainly in the form of OTCs (Officer Training Corps attached to the posher Public Schools. There were the Sea Cadets, but these seemed to be Sea Scouts in long trousers. Thus there was a need, which with the 'Battle of Britain Effect' meant that the inauguration of the ATC caused a stampede. In reality it was an enormous con-trick, it being inferred that membership of the ATC would guarantee you a seat in a Spitfire, this being emphasised by the fact that girls were not accepted since girls did not fly (In the RAF at least).

Actually in all seriousness it was a brilliant idea. It gave the Air Ministry a pool of lads from whom they could pick the best and it helped to prevent the brightest lads being seduced by the other services.

A Squadron of 100 plus was immediately formed, closely followed by two more. There was a surge of fervour in the school to enlist, but the headmaster warned us that we would be coming into contact with boys from inferior schools, not to speak of errand boys and street urchins and that he was forming a Grammar School Squadron, which would form a sort of *Corps*

D'elite a sort of Brigade of Guards among cadets. The obvious flaw in this bold plan was that whereas the 'Town' outfits were led by distinguished ex airman (One was led by Sir Arthur Whitten Brown, you could not get more distinguished than that), we would be led by our dear headmaster whose knowledge of matters martial was limited to doing the Military Two-step, at the Rotary Club dinner-dance. A further problem was that ATC squadrons were sequentially numbered so the town squadrons were in the 200s by the time ours was registered we had to bear the disgrace of a four-figure number.

We had held back on the hinted incentive that we as a school unit would parade in school time, which proved untrue. In addition our 'Officers' comprised some of the least able of our school masters, the only one with any claim was the Geography master who was made Navigation Instructor, presumably on the basis that he would know where places were even if he did not know how to get to them.

I recall farcical attempts to teach Drill on soft grass in Singleton Park – we must have looked like a dysfunctional Brownie pack.

Most disastrous of all, our late registration put us well down the queue for uniforms, we were measured for them all right but by the time we got them we had outgrown them. They were made of the same cloth as real RAF uniforms, but with no side pockets in the tunics, no eagle shoulder badges, chrome instead of brass buttons and were done up to the neck like pre-1935 RAF garb. Now there lay a problem. With trousers shortening the legs or taking in the waist can overcome waist/leg disproportion. Tunic arms or even hems can be shortened but they cannot be lengthened nor can anything be done with the neck. When my uniform did arrive it was ample in the chest but mating the hooks and eyes of the collar called for mechanical assistance. Consequently I strutted about in a near-strangulated condition. In desperation I gave my tunic to a more suitably portioned lad who was still awaiting his, and had been parading in uniform trousers and a check sports jacket.

Happily that state of affairs did not persist for me since I shortly found myself in the University Air Squadron.

This came about by enrolling me in Swansea University to read engineering. This involved re-learning what I already knew about physics, learning something about geology, failing to grasp any aspect whatsoever of calculus and discovering that I was rubbish at engineering drawing Of this latter I had no difficulty in understanding the principles of say, Third Angle Projection, but the finished article appeared to have been created by a dipsomaniac in a coal house. The one solid plus was the opportunity it gave to join the UAS.

The college was then a vastly different place, apart from the recently built library there was besides College House, the Singleton 'Abbey' of the Vivians, there were half a dozen or so temporary sheds. The entire population including the evacuated departments of the University of London and the Department of Explosives

Research (whose location in the basement of the Chemistry building made study of that subject deeply disturbing). There were fewer than 500 on what we would now call the Campus. The students were overwhelmingly male, there was just one female in the Science Faculty and a dozen or so on the Arts side. The solitary Science wench sidled as if in (well justified) fear of serious assault, the Arts women moved around in a tight giggling gaggle. Unlike the men students who carried their books under their arms the women clasped theirs to their burgeoning bosoms. If caught in a shower when moving between buildings these books were transferred from breast to bonce to become impromptu head-coverings so the gaggle resembled a Roman Testudino embarking a siege-assault.

The Common rooms were strictly segregated. The women's was a chintzy boudoir, the men's was like the public bar of a run-down ale house, presumably a familiar ambience for most of the men.

Off duty, as it were the women were confined to the Beck Hall seraglio while the men were accommodated in houses of the Beer, Boarding and possibly Bawdy variety thus socialising took place in Refractory, presumably so named to give an Oxbridge aura to a seedy café. Although the meals were of penitentiary standard, morning coffee was more civilised. Tea as I recall was 1p, coffee was 50% more but the seriously wealthy bought 'Coffee Dashes' at 2p. This milky coffee was desperately weak but it was served in tumblers held in nickel-plated holders that gave an air of considerable sophistication.

Of course admission to the university carried no guarantee of admission into the Hallowed Halls of the Air Squadron. The odds were against it since 'Squadron' was something of an exaggeration, numbers being confined to a dozen or so and two or three of these seemed to be reserved for the London students. I need not have worried most of the freshmen were seeking to avoid call-up and joining the Hole Guard assisted this aim. In addition to a uniform, they were issued with obsolete rifles (fortunately ammunitionless) and big boots which encouraged them to stamp and shout around the place in a most vulgar fashion.

Due I fear to being under subscribed, I was accepted into the Air Squadron and issued with a uniform which was the proper RAF clobber but with ATC buttons and cap badge, plus the shirt and tie which demonstrated our superiority over the Home Guard hooligans. We had to provide our own shoes, one of our number only had brown ones so he had to paint them black. The paint or whatever it was came off when he cleaned them so the repainting had to be redone daily thus he smelt pungently and his trouser bottoms were black.

I do not recall what the Home Guard Officers were like but ours were gentlemen, the Commanding Officer being the elegant and much respected Professor Thomas (Prof Tom) and his sidekick in the English Department 'Tommy Taig' acted as Adjutant as well as teaching navigation. A regular Flight Sergeant Air Gunner who had won a Distinguished Flying Medal (DFM) attempting to bomb the bridge at Maastrict in May 1940. He was being rested from operations and taught us drill,

Morse code and gunnery. There was a proper Orderly Room staffed by an airman waiting commissioning into the Administrative Branch and a civilian lady clerk.

Unlike the Home Guard whose storming and stamping was confined to parades, we could retire to the peace of the UAS cellars to practice, for instance stripping and reassembling a Browning machine-gun against the clock, blindfolded while reciting the litany of the arcane names of the component parts. (e. g. 'Rear sear retainer keeper and spring') – all much less taxing than boring old trigonometry. Just occasionally there was the opportunity to get to RAF Stormy Down and ride in a real genuine (albeit severely obsolete) Whitely bomber. Oddly, although I was destined to serve His Gracious Majesty and later his charming daughter on and off for almost 40 years, I would never aging ride in a real warplane, as opposed to trainers and transport aircraft.

We were 'parented' by the local balloon barrage unit, whose winches and gas-cylinder trailers stood on every patch of flattish open ground, whilst their men and women lived, ate and slept in various houses and halls around the town.

Shortly after joining the UAS one was 'Attested' that is to say actually sworn in as a member of the Armed Forces. This took place at a collection of commandeered houses and such grandly called RAF Penarth. This procedure took a couple of days and thus represented my first sojourn with the RAF. It was not encouraging. One was marched about and shouted at and one's most precious parts were closely inspected. One stood about, one was fed with vile concoctions and slept on an uncomfortable bed. I say slept but in fact it took an age to drift off so no sooner had one done so than an uncouth little man made a frightful noise and obscenely shouted,

'Hands off c***s, feet in socks!'

It seemed extraordinary that chaps that had offered themselves so generously should be greeted with such discourtesy. I hoped that it was all part of a cunning plan to discourage all but the most blindly dedicated, and that being shouted at by horrible little men in the pre-dawn chill was not normal RAF routine. This hope was to remain unfulfilled.

Anyway after two days one was sent home with a tiny badge that enabled the less myopic to identified one as a member of His Majesty's Royal Air Force.

The real culture shock came when visiting RAF Fairwood Common. For much of 1940 a stream of lorries had conveyed copper slag from the great mountains of waste in the Lower Swansea Valley, through the town and out to Gower.

There was naturally no official opening, one day one realised that the lorries had stopped and the planes had started. The South Road was closed but one could observe matters from the top of Kittle lane and from the North Road. It all seemed so peaceful, occasionally a Defiant or a Whirlwind would take off and in between apart from the sounds of an engine being run up, all seemed tranquil. One might spot the odd vehicle, maybe even a person, unhurriedly walking.

When as part of the UAS we actually went there, it was like turning over a stone or kicking an anthill, the place so tranquil from a distance was a teeming mass of men and women intent upon urgent tasks. Well perhaps not always that urgent.

Exciting? Of course it was exciting, mingling with the aircrew, seeing the mighty Beaufighters taking off and to wander round the hangers where they were being taken to bits. Visiting the armoury, the radio section and so on. The parachute packers ('If it doesn't open we'll give you another free of charge') Visiting the Control Tower (Where 20 years later I would officiate). Everything was exciting except perhaps the queues for everything. Those queues could have been a turn off were it not for the thrill of feeling the UAS's very own Moth Minor react to the controls.

That was at Summer Camp when we ate and slept and really experienced service life, not always an unalloyed pleasure. Indeed it was for most of us our first experience of mixing with adults on equal terms, having a laugh, having a moan, exchanging risqué banter with both men and women. I certainly felt that I had been thrown in at the deep end and would prepare me for the day when that (ominously single) Railway warrant landed on the mat.

I joined that train with a 10/- (50p) note in my pocket, which had been pressed into my hand by Annie King's Head, the Gore Terrace maid with a tearful hug and an enjoiner to 'Come back safe'. It probably represented most of a week's wages. She was a kind, generous but I fear exploited, soul.